S0-DZD-386

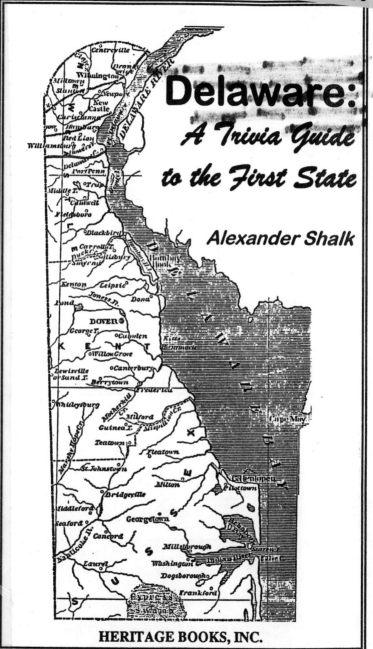

Delaware:

A Trivia Guide
to the First State

Alexander Shalk

HERITAGE BOOKS, INC.

Del
917.51
SHA

Copyright 1995
Alexander Shalk

Published 1995 By

HERITAGE BOOKS, INC.
1540E Pointer Ridge Place, Bowie, MD 20716
1-800-398-7709

ISBN 0-7884-0352-4

A Complete Catalog Listing Hundreds of Titles
On History, Genealogy, and Americana
Available Free Upon Request

To

Christine and Benjamin

Table of Contents

Delaware People

Introduction

The questions in this book were written as a celebration of Delaware's rich cultural and historical heritage. Readers who keep abreast of local news, have travelled the state, and perhaps have even read a history book or two should have no trouble answering many of these questions. Many questions, however, are written to challenge even the most ardent Delaware enthusiasts.

This book would not have been possible without the writings of such distinguished Delaware historians as John A. Munroe, Harold H. Hancock, Carol A. Hoffecker, and William H. Williams. Their work has taught me a great deal about our state's shining moments as well as its darker ones.

I also have our journalists and newspapers to thank. Few days go by without a feature story about a noteworthy Delawarean in statewide publications such as the *News Journal*, the *Delaware State News*, or in local weeklies. Older Delawareans will remember such columnists as W. Emerson Wilson, Betty Burroughs, and William P. Frank who wrote with fervor about Delaware subjects.

I am grateful to a number of people who helped me bring this project to fruition. Janet W. Garrett, Smyrna High School business department chairperson, formatted, typed, and edited most of the text with the able assistance of her student Cathy Steele.

Jack Ireland, sports editor for the *News Journal*; Susan A. Biro, former editor of the *Smyrna-Clayton Sun*; and John P. Reid, publisher of *Collecting Delaware Books*, a newsletter, were all kind enough to read sections of the text and offer advice.

John Dickinson, retired Smyrna High School librarian, read the entire manuscript and offered invaluable advice. I am also grateful to John for being the first to introduce me to the significance of Delaware history and books.

Dr. John A. Munroe, H. Rodney Sharp Professor Emeritus of the University of Delaware, suggested important corrections. It was an honor to have such a distinguished historian read the manuscript. I am deeply grateful to him.

Karen Ackermann, president of Heritage Books, Inc., deserves my gratitude for believing in this project from the beginning. I am also grateful to Lisa M. Hooper, assistant editor for Heritage Books, Inc., for her thorough reading of the manuscript. Her suggestions proved invaluable.

Finally, a deep appreciation goes to my wonderful wife, Christine, whose editing skills and encouragement made this book possible.

The questions are arranged so there are logical sequences to the sections, particularly in the county sections which are arranged as tours. The history sections are arranged by date, and the government sections have questions that are grouped by topic. The questions about people are generally grouped by topic or the era during which the people lived.

This book can, of course, be read alone, but it may even be more enjoyable when used with friends in jeopardy, quiz bowl, or trivia-style games.

What's so special about Delaware?--everything! Have fun testing your knowledge of Delaware as you read *Delaware: A Trivia Guide to the First State*.

Delaware's Counties

New Castle County Tour

Although it's the smallest county in the second smallest state, New Castle County is big enough to boast of two distinct geographic regions. The northern portion of the county is part of the rolling hills of the Appalachian Piedmont, out of which flows the scenic Brandywine River, whose current once powered colonial waterwheels. South of the piedmont, in a line that roughly follows Newark to Wilmington, New Castle County becomes part of the Atlantic coastal plain--an area of traditionally rich farmland that is now in the throes of suburban expansion.

During Delaware's colonial period, New Castle County's land, river, proximity to Philadelphia, and access to the Delaware Bay all conspired to make the county Delaware's most populous. Within 150 years after the arrival of the Swedes--Delaware's first successful European settlers--thriving colonial towns and productive farms dotted the landscape, the most distinctive town being then, as now, the town of New Castle. By the nineteenth century, New Castle County began to take its present shape as Wilmington wrestled the county seat from New Castle and laid claim as the industrial and urban center of the state--thanks largely to the du Ponts and other entrepreneurs who realized the economic significance of the union of the Brandywine and Christina Rivers.

Today, what characterizes New Castle County is a mix of urban and suburban life. Wilmington--long referred to as the "Chemical Capital of the World"--now qualifies as a major banking center and corporate center in the United States. Surrounding Wilmington are suburban areas that, if not notable for their planning, furnish residents with commuter fundamentals: malls, schools, and single family homes. Below the canal, Middletown earns a reputation as the fastest growing area in the state. Like all counties whose resources have been stretched to their limits, New Castle County faces the challenge of preserving its beauties, yet accommodating a population that has been steadily growing since World War II.

We will begin our trivia journey in the town of New Castle, where William Penn arrived in 1681 to claim his title to Pennsylvania and "The Three Counties Upon the Delaware."

1. From Battery Park in New Castle you can look out over a wide expanse of the Delaware River and see the Delaware Memorial Bridge. The bridge is a memorial to servicemen and women of which war?
    a. the Civil War
    b. the Spanish-American War
    c. World War I
    d. World War II

2. The colonial homes of New Castle rival the best of the colonial homes in the original thirteen colonies, particularly a New Castle house that was finished by a Delaware lawyer and statesman whose father signed the Declaration of Independence and the U.S. Constitution. What is the name of this late Georgian-style house?
    a. the Ryves Holt House
    b. the George Read II House
    c. the Loockerman House
    d. the Cummins House

3. When William Penn received his grant of Pennsylvania from Charles I in 1681, his grant did not include the three counties of Delaware which were at the time owned by the Duke of York. To separate the Duke's lands from Penn's, an arc surveyed from New Castle became the boundary line. How many miles is the radius of this arc?
    a. 5 b. 12 c. 21 d. 36

4. Years later the arc was measured by professional surveyors who used the spire of what building in New Castle to complete the measurement?
    a. New Castle Court House   c. Old Dutch House
    b. Old Town Hall   d. Immanuel Church

3

DELAWARE: A TRIVIA GUIDE

5. Built in 1703, the Immanuel Episcopal Church on The Green was restored after a 1980 fire. The church was the first parish of the Church of England in Delaware. Name the English king who started the Church of England.
   a. George III
   b. Henry VIII
   c. Edward VI
   d. Charles I

6. A house on Third Street across from The Green was built around 1700 when New Castle was an English colony. It is, however, considered an excellent example of the architecture of New Castle's first settlers who were not English. What is the name of this house?
   a. Old German House
   b. Old Swedes House
   c. Old Dutch House
   d. Old French House

7. Let's leave the town of New Castle via Route 273 and drive west until we intersect with Route 40 at Hare's Corner. Route 40, from State Road to the Maryland line, is named after a Revolutionary War hero who is noted for helping train the cavalry of the Continental Army. What is the name of this Polish officer?
   a. Thaddeus Kusciusko
   b. Marquis de Lafayette
   c. Casimir Pulaski
   d. Friedrich von Steuben

8. The New Castle County Airport (Route 40 near Hare's) services private and charter flights and is the home of the Delaware Air National Guard. It has also served as a testing sight of an aircraft that can fly like a helicopter and a plane. What is the name of this experimental aircraft?
   a. the Osprey
   b. the Eagle
   c. the Falcon
   d. the Dodo

4

9. Let's head further west on Route 273 and take I-95 north into Wilmington. South of the city, I-95--known as the Kennedy Memorial Highway--intersects with I-495, an eastern bypass around Wilmington. I-495 is dedicated to veterans of which war?
    a. Revolutionary War
    b. Civil War
    c. World War II
    d. Vietnam War

10. The Wilmington Marine Terminal (off I-495 on Route 9) is located on the south bank of which river?
    a. St. Jones
    b. Murderkill
    c. Brandywine
    d. Christina

11. No other port in the world imports more of a certain type of fruit than does the Wilmington Marine Terminal. What is this fruit?
    a. orange
    b. apple
    c. banana
    d. kiwi

12. As you take Route 13 into Wilmington, you'll pass the Wilmington Train Station. Built in a Romanesque style, the station was designed by the firm of what noted architect?
    a. Frank Lloyd Wright
    b. Richard M. Hunt
    c. Louis Henri Sullivan
    d. Frank Furness

13. Which railroad built the Station in 1906?
    a. Pennsylvania   c. Delaware
    b. Amtrack   d. Baltimore and Ohio

14. Baseball fans were thrilled when the Daniel S. Frawley Stadium opened in April of 1993 with minor league baseball. Who is the field named after?
    a. William Julius Johnson
    b. Harmon Carey
    c. James Sills
    d. Clifford Brown

15. Old Swedes Church, the oldest continuously operating church in Delaware, sits at the corner of Church and Seventh streets in Wilmington. Built by Swedish Delawareans in 1698, the church is now officially called Holy Trinity and houses an Episcopalian congregation. What was the original religious denomination of Old Swedes?
    a. Catholic
    b. Lutheran
    c. Baptist
    d. Methodist

16. It's fitting that the "Swedish Nightingale" sang in Old Swedes Church when she toured America in the middle of the nineteenth century. Name the famous actress.
    a. Christine Nilsson
    b. Maria Malibran
    c. Beverly Sills
    d. Jenny Lind

17. Nearby at the foot of Seventh Street in Wilmington is a black-granite obelisk--a gift given by the Swedish in 1938 to commemorate the three-hundredth anniversary of the Swedish landing at "The Rocks." A sculpture of which of the following sits on top of the monument?
    a. Queen Christina
    b. Fort Christina
    c. *Kalmar Nyckel*
    d. Lenni Lenape Indians

18. Let's go to the heart of Wilmington--Rodney Square. There you'll find a statue of Caesar Rodney, which commemorates his famous ride to Philadelphia in 1776 to cast his vote for independence. What term denotes a statue consisting of a horse and rider?

  a. statuette   c. equestrian
  b. relief sculpture   d. horseback

19. On Rodney Square is the Hotel du Pont, a world class hotel with highly regarded restaurants and accommodations. It also has a theater completely enclosed within the hotel. What is the name of this theater?

  a. Three Little Bakers
  b. the Playhouse
  c. the Everett
  d. the Grand Opera House

20. We'll now head south from Rodney Square down Wilmington's Market Street, which is now a mall. Located on the Market Street Mall at Ninth Street is the F. W. Woolworth Building, which was built in 1940 in a popular architectural style of that period. Which term describes this architectural style which emphasizes geometric forms?

  a. Art Deco
  b. Georgian
  c. Gothic
  d. Victorian

21. Constructed in the 1870s in the Second Empire style, the Grand Opera House, with its mansard roof and elaborate facade, is a masterpiece of Victorian design. The traditionally secretive group that built the Grand Opera House still holds meetings on the second floor. Who built the Grand Opera House?

  a. Moose   c. Masonic Order
  b. Odd Fellows   d. Delaware Saengerbund

7

22. Between Seventh and Eighth streets is an arts center that was once located in Wilmington's East Side where it served as a haven for local African-American artists, musicians, and dancers who taught and performed there. The center relocated downtown to a building with three times the space to expand its horizons. What is the name of this center?
   a. Delaware Center for the Contemporary Arts
   b. Delaware Theatre Company
   c. Wilmington Drama League
   d. Christina Cultural Arts Center

23. On Market Street, between Fifth and Sixth, is Wilmington's Old Town Hall. Begun shortly before the start of the nineteenth century, this Federal-style building housed the city's government until World War I. At the top of the building is a decorative dome-shaped structure that looks similar to a gazebo. What is this decorative piece called?
   a. belfry
   b. widow's walk
   c. spire
   d. cupola

24. On the same block of Market, you'll find an enclave of eighteenth-century houses that were moved there to save them from demolition. What is this enclave called?
   a. Willingtown Square
   b. The Green
   c. Rodney Village
   d. The Strand

25. Let's take Fourth Street west into the heart of Wilmington's Hispanic community. Wilmington's non-native born Hispanics are mostly from what self-governing dependency of the United States?
   a. Puerto Rico   c. Mexico
   b. Cuba   d. Chile

26. On Sixth and West sits the oldest Roman Catholic Church in Delaware (built in 1816). What is the name of this church?
    a. Saint Matthew's
    b. Saint Elizabeth's
    c. Saint Peter's
    d. Saint Paul's

27. Just south of Wilmington's Hispanic community is Browntown, the city's Polish community. Built by the Polish community, the impressive spires of St. Hedwig's Roman Catholic Church can be seen from I-95. In what style suggestive of the Medieval period is the church built?
    a. French Provincial
    b. Dutch Colonial
    c. Gothic
    d. Classical

28. Many Delawareans and out-of-staters enjoy the food and festivities at St. Anthony's Festival which takes place every June in the heart of Wilmington's Little Italy. St. Anthony, the church's patron saint, is associated with which city in Italy?
    a. Padua
    b. Naples
    c. Venice
    d. Milan

29. Although it is the largest, St. Anthony's is not the only ethnic festival in Wilmington. Nearby at the Greek Orthodox Church, Greek Delawareans hold a festival a week prior to St. Anthony's. Greeks trace their religious roots back to 1054 when the Great Schism resulted in a split in the Christian Church. Rome became the center of the Roman Catholic Church. What city became the center of the Eastern Orthodox Church?
    a. Athens
    b. Baghdad
    c. Cairo
    d. Constantinople

9

30. Saint Ann's sits in the heart of what was traditionally the Irish community on the east side of Delaware Avenue. Many of the Irish who migrated to Delaware in the 1840s took jobs in the DuPont powder mills. Why did so many Irish leave Ireland during that time period?
    a. for political freedom
    b. to buy property
    c. the potato famine
    d. for religious freedom

31. The Delaware Art Museum (north of the Italian community on Kentmere Parkway) is noted, in part, for Howard Pyle's works and a collection of paintings donated by art patron Samuel Bancroft, Jr. These paintings include works by artists Dante Gabriel Rossetti and William Leigh Hunt who are collectively grouped under what title?
    a. Realists
    b. Pre-Raphaelite
    c. Ashcan
    d. Expressionist

32. Completed in 1901, built of granite, and having an observation deck, one of the most striking water towers in the country sits in which Wilmington park?
    a. Rockford
    b. Banning
    c. Brandywine Creek
    d. Bellevue

33. Let's leave Wilmington proper and head north on I-95. As you cross the Brandywine River you'll pass over a zoo established by Wilmington philantropist Samuel H. Baynard and other interested citizens. Name the zoo.
    a. Baynard Zoo   c. Brandywine Zoo
    b. Wilmington Zoo   d. New Castle County Zoo

34. A sizeable Jewish community was once centered near P. S. du Pont Elementary School on Thirty-Fourth and Van Buren. The three major branches of modern Judaism--conservative, orthodox, and reformed--are represented in New Castle County. Rabbis are, of course, Jewish religious leaders. What does Rabbi mean?
    a. minister
    b. teacher
    c. holy man
    d. spiritual leader

35. A few miles outside the city is Bellevue State Park. Located in Bellevue is a house that was once owned by William du Pont from 1928 - 1965. He had the house altered to look like Montpelier in Virginia. Whose house was Montpelier?
    a. Thomas Jefferson
    b. Benjamin Franklin
    c. George Washington
    d. James Madison

36. Further up I-95 is a town that was founded in 1900 by artists, writers, actors, and single-tax advocates who envisioned the town as a utopia for the creative. What is the name of the town?
    a. Claymont   c. Hockessin
    b. Arden   d. Belleview

37. As we swing northwest off of I-95 we enter the hilly area of the Brandywine Valley. Because of the large estates built by the du Ponts and other wealthy Delawareans, this area--particularly around Greenville--has a nickname. What is this name?
    a. Snob Hill
    b. Chateau Country
    c. Brandywine Valley
    d. Castle Cribs

38. Here's a geography question. The region that marks the division between the piedmont and the low-lying coastal plain passes through Newark and Wilmington. What is the geographical term for this type of region?
    a. fall line
    b. plateau
    c. tree line
    d. estuary

39. Founded as a museum by Henry Francis du Pont in 1951, the Winterthur Museum on Route 52 houses an internationally famous collection of American decorative art and furniture. Winterthur also hosts what horse race every year in May?
    a. Winterthur Harness
    b. Winterthur Thoroughbred
    c. Winterthur Point-to-Point
    d. Winterthur Polo

40. The Delaware Museum of Natural History on Route 52 proudly displays a 500 pound clam and the largest egg of its kind in the world. What kind of egg is it?
    a. elephant
    b. fish
    c. snake
    d. bird

41. Nearby on Route 141 is a museum that is the site of the du Pont gunpowder mills. What is this museum called?
    a. Iron Hill
    b. Hagley
    c. Rockwood
    d. Winterthur

42. Just down the road on Rockland Road is Nemours Mansion--a Louis XVI-style chateau replete with formal French gardens. (Also on the estate is the Alfred I. du Pont Institute.) Built by Alfred I. du Pont between 1909 - 1910, the estate is surrounded by a nine-foot high wall topped by what?
    a. spikes
    b. barbed wire
    c. shards of glass
    d. rocks

43. The highest point in Delaware is 442 feet about sea level. On what road near Centerville is the highest point?
    a. Snuff Mill
    b. Ebright
    c. Old Capitol Trail
    d. Lancaster Pike

44. If you take Route 82 west, you will eventually cross over Hoopes Reservoir. Hoopes has Delaware's only astronomical observatory. What is the name of this observatory?
    a. Mt. Cuba
    b. Iron Hill
    c. Ashland
    d. Montchanin

45. Let's cross the state line into Pennsylvania by taking Route 100 north to U.S. Route 1. A bit east is Chadds Ford, the site of the Battle of the Brandywine where George Washington was defeated by which British general?
    a. Benedict Arnold
    b. Lord Cornwallis
    c. William Howe
    d. John Burgoyne

46. South on Route 1 is Longwood Gardens--internationally noted for its conservatories and outdoor gardens. In the arboretum visitors are often delighted by a collection of dwarf trees associated with Japan. What are they called?
    a. topiary
    b. bonsai
    c. origami
    d. bamboo

47. Nearby is the Brandywine River Museum--a restored mill which as part of its collection displays paintings by three generations of this famous family. Who are they?
    a. Hesselius
    b. Wyeth
    c. Shaw
    d. Pyle

48. Near the Ashland Nature Center on Brackenville Road is a rare type of bridge. Which type is it?
    a. suspension
    b. steel
    c. drawbridge
    d. covered

49. A few miles away is a village and surrounding area that many say has developed beyond its capacity. The Indian name for the village is "place of many foxes." Name this village.
    a. Woodenhawk
    b. Appoquinimink
    c. Hockessin
    d. Mispillion

50. A number of roads in Delaware were originally privately constructed toll roads called turnpikes, many of which were constructed during the Colonial Period. Included among these are Route 48 (the Lancaster Pike) and Route 52 (the Kennett Pike). As we head southwest down Route 2, the Kirkwood Highway (named after Robert Kirkwood, a Revolutionary war hero), we will cross over Route 41, another former turnpike. What is the name of this road?
    a. Concord Pike
    b. Limestone Road
    c. Kennett Pike
    d. Newport-Gap Pike

51. Let's take the Kirkwood Highway into Newark. On White Clay Creek in Newark is a paper mill that is noted for its production of fine paper. What is the name of this mill?
    a. Curtis
    b. Rodney
    c. Dickinson
    d. McKean

52. The murder of a student during a fracas in 1858 played a large role in closing down Newark College--the predecessor to the University of Delaware--until 1869. On the steps of what building did this murder occur?
    a. Mitchell Hall
    b. Purnell Hall
    c. Old College
    d. Memorial

53. Legend has it that the author of "The Raven" stayed at the Deerpark--the University of Delaware's watering hole. What is the name of this famous poet?
    a. Edgar Allan Poe
    b. Emily Dickinson
    c. Ralph Waldo Emerson
    b. Robert Frost

54. If you enjoy hearing local and national rock and roll acts, you can go to the Stone Balloon. What literary term describes the juxtaposition of two words that don't normally go together such as in the case of the Stone Balloon?
   a. personification
   b. oxymoron
   c. onomatopoeia
   d. alliteration

55. Newark High School's school name is the Yellowjackets. What are the school names for Christiana and Glasgow--two other local high schools?
   a. the Vikings and the Dragons
   b. the Eagles and the Highlanders
   c. the Senators and the Rams
   d. the Wildcats and the Colonials

56. Many Delawareans--including those who are not of German descent--enjoy the yearly Octoberfest put on by this German club located in Ogletown. Name this club.
   a. Saengerbund
   b. Bauernstube
   c. Liebraumilch
   d. Turnesverein

57. You can play "golf" in Walter S. Carpenter, Jr. State Park (two miles north of Newark off Route 896), but don't bother to bring clubs. What type of golf can you play?
   a. putt putt
   b. frisbee
   c. LPGA
   d. amateur

58. In 1981, Chrysler was bailed out of financial trouble in Delaware with a loan from the state. Chrysler was able to quickly pay off the loan because of the success of the LeBaron and what other car built in the 1980s?
   a. Cordova
   b. LeMans
   c. Accord
   d. K-car

59. Not far from I-95 off Route 896 is Cooch's Bridge--the site of Delaware's only Revolutionary War battle (skirmish is a better word). Tradition has it that this was where this flag was first unfurled. Which flag?
   a. Washington's colors
   b. Delaware
   c. Stars and Stripes
   d. Union Jack

60. Off Route 896 before Summit Bridge is the largest inland body of water in Delaware. What is the name of this body of water?
   a. Voshell Pond
   b. Trap Pond
   c. Lums Pond
   d. Hearns Pond

61. If you follow Route 896 south you'll arrive in Middletown. Scenes from the 1989 movie *The Dead Poets Society*, starring Robin Williams, were filmed at what theatre in Middletown?
   a. Chapel Street
   b. Delaware Children's Theatre
   c. Everett
   d. Candlelight Dinner Theatre

62. Many of the beautiful Victorian homes in Middletown were built during the second half of the nineteenth century by farmers who profited from a type of fruit that Delaware was noted for until disease ruined the crop. What is this fruit?
    a. coconut
    b. apples
    c. peaches
    d. pears

63. About a mile south on Route 896 out of Middletown is a picturesque colonial church dating back to 1768. What is its name?
    a. St. Anne's
    b. Welsh Tract
    c. African Methodist Episcopal
    d. Camden Meeting

64. Down a side road is a private school on Noxontown Pond dating back to 1929. Name this school.
    a. Tower Hill
    b. St. Andrew's
    c. Padua
    d. Caravel

65. A few miles down the road from Townsend is what state forest?
    a. Woodland Beach
    b. Redden
    c. Blackbird
    d. Ellendale

66. Legend has it that Blackbird Creek is named after which famous pirate whose nickname was Blackbeard?
    a. Edward Teach
    b. Jean Laffite
    c. Benjamin Hornigold
    d. William Kidd

67. Route 896 is only one major way to get to southern New Castle County. Let's double back and take Route 13 south, starting near the junction of Route 13 and Route 40. We'll start at a State of Delaware conference site that was once the home of John Middleton Clayton who, among his many accomplishments, was a Delaware chief justice, a United States senator, and secretary of state to Zachary Taylor. What is the name of Clayton's former home?
    a. The Hermitage
    b. Mordington
    c. Buena Vista
    d. The Homestead

68. Follow Route 13 to Route 72 and take Route 72 a few miles to Delaware City--a town whose nineteenth-century developer wrongly thought would boom because of the canal traffic. Off Delaware City in the Delaware River is an island that served as a union prisoner-of-war camp (Fort Delaware) where 2,400 were thought to have perished during the Civil War. Name the island.
    a. Point of Cedars
    b. Sand
    c. Pea Patch
    d. Reedy

69. The death toll at Fort Delaware was so high that it was often referred to as the Andersonville of the North. In what state was Andersonville, a notorious prisoner-of-war camp?
    a. Alabama
    b. Georgia
    c. Tennessee
    d. North Carolina

70. What bridge can you take to cross the canal on Route 9 at Delaware City?
    a. Indian River Inlet
    b. Summit
    c. Reedy Point
    d. St. Georges

71. Route 13 crosses the Chesapeake and Delaware Canal at what city?
    a. St. Georges
    b. Summit
    c. Delaware City
    d. Kirkwood

72. Continuing south you'll see Drawyer's Church, a beautiful brick church that was begun in 1773. What is the denomination of Drawyer's?
    a. Catholic
    b. Methodist
    c. Presbyterian
    d. Baptist

73. Route 13 goes through Odessa. Odessa was named after a city in what country?
    a. Germany
    b. France
    c. England
    d. Ukraine

74. Many early Delaware cities were named after local residents who could afford to construct bridges across nearby streams and creeks thus easing the difficulties of colonial travel. What was Odessa's original name?
    a. Fleming's Landing
    b. Cantwell's Bridge
    c. Johnnycake Landing
    d. Taylor's Bridge

75. Odessa was also once an important river port for wheat, corn, and tobacco before the railroad in Middletown took the business. Name the river that goes through Odessa and eventually empties into the Delaware River.
    a. Indian
    b. St. Jones
    c. Smyrna
    d. Appoquinimink

76. Visitors to the Corbit-Sharp House in Odessa are often impressed by the exterior and interior beauty of the mid-Georgian architecture of the home (built by local tanner William Corbit). Who now owns and operates the Corbit-Sharp House?
 a. Delaware Tourism Office
 b. The Historical Society of Delaware
 c. Winterthur
 d. Hagley

77. In the drawing room of the Corbit-Sharp House is a Waterford crystal chandelier and a tall clock built by what nationally renowned Delaware clock maker?
 a. Eli Terry
 b. Christian Huygens
 c. Benjamin Banneker
 d. Duncan Beard

78. From southern New Castle County it's hard to miss the cooling towers of the nuclear power plant in New Jersey. In what county is the plant located?
 a. Cape May
 b. Salem
 c. Somerset
 d. Burlington

New Castle County Tour Answers

1. d. World War II

2. b. George Read II House

3. b. 12

4. a. New Castle Court House

5. b. Henry VIII

6. c. Old Dutch House

7. c. Casimir Pulaski

8. a. the Osprey

9. d. Vietnam War

10. d. Christina

11. c. banana

12. d. Frank Furness

13. a. Pennsylvania

14. a. William Julius Johnson

15. b. Lutheran

16. d. Jenny Lind

17. c. *Kalmar Nyckel*

18. c. equestrian

19. b. the Playhouse

20. a. Art Deco

21. c. Masonic Order

22. d. Christina Cultural Arts Center

23. d. cupola

24. a. Willingtown Square

25. a. Puerto Rico

26. c. Saint Peter's

27. c. Gothic

28. a. Padua

29. d. Constantinople

30. c. the potato famine

31. b. Pre-Raphaelite

32. a. Rockford

33. c. Brandywine Zoo

34. b. teacher

35. d. James Madison

36. b. Arden

37. b. Chateau Country

38. a. fall line

39. c. Winterthur Point-to-Point

40. d. bird

41. b. Hagley

42. c. shards of glass

43. b. Ebright

44. a. Mt. Cuba

45. c. William Howe

46. b. bonsai

47. b. Wyeth

48. d. covered

49. c. Hockessin

50. d. Newport-Gap Pike

51. a. Curtis

52. c. Old College

53. a. Edgar Allan Poe

54. b. oxymoron

55. a. the Vikings and the Dragons

56.   a.   Saengerbund

57.   b.   frisbee

58.   d.   K-car

59.   c.   Stars and Stripes

60.   c.   Lums Pond

61.   c.   Everett

62.   c.   peaches

63.   a.   St. Anne's

64.   b.   St. Andrew's

65.   c.   Blackbird

66.   a.   Edward Teach

67.   c.   Buena Vista

68.   c.   Pea Patch

69.   b.   Georgia

70.   c.   Reedy Point

71.   a.   St. Georges

72.   c.   Presbyterian

73.   d.   Ukraine

74.   b.   Cantwell's Bridge

75. d. Appoquinimink

76. c. Winterthur

77. d. Duncan Beard

78. b. Salem

Kent County Tour

William Penn didn't take long to stake his claim to Kent County. When he arrived at the town of New Castle in 1682, one of his first official acts was to give Delaware's middle county of St. Jones its new name of Kent, after Kent County, England. Soon after, Penn ordered the laying out of Dover as the county seat in a grid design similar to Philadelphia's, although his plans didn't become a reality until 1717.

Because of its central location, Dover was an excellent choice for a county seat. And largely because of the St. Jones River and its easy access to the Bay, it didn't take long for Dover to grow into a thriving colonial market and trading center. In 1777, Dover became the capital of the state less by design than by a quirk of fate. After the British defeated Washington at the Battle of the Brandywine, the British troops occupied Wilmington, making it dangerous for the General Assembly to meet in nearby New Castle. Thus the Assembly voted to meet in Dover and, of course, has been there ever since.

Dover now vies with Wilmington as a major urban center in the state. The city is home to Dover Air Force Base, textile and food processing industries, masterful colonial architecture, and a slew of strip malls along Route 13.

Surrounding Dover from the northern county line near Smyrna to the southern terminus through Milford, lie small towns, housing developments, and farmland. Slow to develop Kent County's agricultural potential in the county's early history, Kent farmers are today major suppliers to local food processing industries including the Delmarva Peninsula's pride--poultry. Along Kent's coastal communities watermen still ply the bay for shellfish, although no longer in the numbers they used to.

We will begin the Kent County journey just north of Smyrna where New Castle County and Kent County are separated by a river that was important to the development of Smyrna.

1. On Route 13, as you pass from New Castle County to Kent County, you have to cross over a river that is part of the county line. What is the name of this river?
    a. Nanticoke
    b. Smyrna
    c. St. Jones
    d. Murderkill

2. Part of Kent County, Maryland, is contiguous to Kent County, Delaware. What other Maryland County is contiguous to Kent County, Delaware?
    a. Queen Anne's
    b. Talbot
    c. Cecil
    d. Dorchester

3. Heading south, the first town in Kent is Smyrna. As it was in the nineteenth century, Smyrna is still an agriculturally productive rural community. Smyrna, however, did not become Smyrna until 1806 when it changed its name. What was its original name?
    a. Duck Creek Crossroads
    b. Smyrna Station
    c. Mifflin's Crossroads
    d. Grogtown

4. Just outside of downtown Smyrna on North Main Street is The Lindens, a seventeenth-century brick home built by a local miller. Its charm relies heavily on a type of roof with two slopes on the sides--the top one less sloped than the bottom. What type of roof is it?
    a. gambrel
    b. mansard
    c. hip
    d. deck

5. Enoch Spruance was a local merchant in Smyrna whose home was built before 1791. For a time it served as the only bank between Wilmington and Dover. It sits on a street whose name delineates its original purpose. What is the name?
   a. Wall
   b. Commerce
   c. Bank
   d. Market

6. The Delaware Railroad, a north-south route, was built in 1856 to help southern Delaware farmers get their goods to markets. Because of the noise and general disruption, some Smyrna residents didn't want the railroad to go directly through town. Instead the line was built a few miles west. Name the town that grew up around the Smyrna depot.
   a. Kenton
   b. Cheswold
   c. Clayton
   d. Harrington

7. Who owns and operates the Delaware Railroad today?
   a. Amtrak
   b. Conrail
   c. Septa
   d. Maryland and Delaware

8. Past Smyrna, the main rail line heads south. In 1882, a line was built off the main line toward Maryland. Then called the Chesapeake and Delaware line, it is now called the Maryland and Delaware line. What two towns in Delaware sprang up around this line?
   a. Camden and Wyoming
   b. Greenwood and Bridgeville
   c. Ellendale and Milton
   d. Kenton and Hartly

9. According to Delaware historian Harold B. Hancock, the original names of this Kent County railroad town named after station agent, William Hart, include Butterpat, Butterpot, Arthursville, and Hawking Corner. Name the town.
    a. Hardscrabble   c. Hartly
    b. Hartford   d. Williamsburg

10. On the east side of Route 13 in Smyrna is the former home of Thomas Collins who was the state's governor during the ratification of the federal constitution. What is the name of this distinctive three-story Georgian brick home?
    a. Belmont Hall
    b. Mordington
    c. Tharp House
    d. Cochran Grange

11. To the east of Smyrna is Bombay Hook. Part of the Atlantic Flyway, Bombay Hook is a National Wildlife Refuge and a national treasure in Delaware's backyard. Bombay Hook is an anglicanization of the word Bompties Hook. From what language does the word come?
    a. English
    b. Swedish
    c. Dutch
    d. Spanish

12. Bombay Hook, most of which is tidal salt marsh, is a stopping point for many species of migratory birds. Birds in distress, particularly rare birds, may be transported to Newark where they will be helped by an organization that has become internationally known for its work with wildlife. What is the name of this organization?
    a. Audubon Society
    b. National Wildlife Refuge System
    c. Tri-State Bird Rescue and Research Center
    d. Environmental Protection Agency

13. Bombay Hook is affected by the rise and fall of the tides. What is the geological term for waters affected by the tides?
    a. estuary
    b. wetlands
    c. inlet
    d. polder

14. On the grounds of Bombay Hook is a Queen-Anne style country house that was built around 1753 by a French Huguenot. What is the name of this house?
    a. Ashland Mills
    b. Linden Hill
    c. Ridgely House
    d. Allee House

15. Postcards show that Augustine Beach and Woodland Beach were once popular resort towns. Visitors might take the *Thomas Clyde* from Philadelphia to spend the day on a Delaware beach. What was the *Thomas Clyde*?
    a. bus
    b. train
    c. steam boat
    d. clipper ship

16. Let's head south along Route 13. South of Smyrna proper you'll pass Lake Como. Lake Como is named after a city in what country?
    a. Italy   c. France
    b. Spain   d. Germany

17. You've passed this eighteen-hole golf course, on Route 13, many times. Name it.
    a. Old Landing Golf Course
    b. Ed "Porky" Oliver Golf Course
    c. Wilmington Country Club
    d. Garrisons Lake Golf Club

18. The next town is Cheswold, the original home of a group of people who have unique racial characteristics. What are these people called?

a. Bedouins   c. Berbers

b. Basques   d. Moors

19. Cheswold was given its name in a contest in 1888 because its original name, Moortown, caused some confusion with other towns of the same name. Chess was decided on because of a stand of chestnut trees near the depot. What does "wold," an Old English word, mean?

a. town

b. forest

c. world

d. land

20. To the east of Cheswold is Leipsic (pronounced Lipsic). If you get to know a resident you might get invited to a "marsh rabbit" dinner. What is a marsh rabbit?

a. deer

b. muskrat

c. goose

d. fox

21. Leipsic was named after a European town known for its fur trade. In what European country is the town?

a. Austria

b. Spain

c. France

d. Germany

22. Further south on Route 13 is Dover, the capital of the state. Dover didn't become the capital officially until 1781 when the capital was transferred from what town?

a. Lewes   c. New Castle

b. Newark   d. Milford

23. Just before Delaware State University on Route 13 is a campus of Delaware Technical and Community College. The College opened in 1966 at its main campus in Georgetown. Under what governor's administration was the school started?
    a. Charles L. Terry
    b. Elbert N. Carvel
    c. Walter W. Bacon
    d. Sherman W. Tribbitt

24. Nearby is the POLYTECH Adult Education building. After completing the required credits, students can receive a diploma that is named after the state's first superintendent of schools. Name him.
    a. James H. Groves
    b. Willard Hall
    c. George S. Messersmith
    d. S. M. Stouffer

25. William H. Delauder--an African American--is currently Delaware State University's president. Name the first black president of the land grant college.
    a. Pauline A. Young
    b. W. C. Jason
    c. Edwina Kruse
    d. Absalom Jones

26. Delaware State University changed its name from Delaware State College in 1993 to better reflect the school's growth. Who has the power to change the name of a state-supported school?
    a. City Council
    b. the Board of Trustees
    c. the Governor
    d. the General Assembly

27. Delaware State University has fielded excellent sports teams, particularly in basketball and football. What is the team name of Delaware State?
    a. Warriors
    b. Blue Hens
    c. Hornets
    d. Vikings

28. There are five public school districts in Kent County. One is the Capital School District in Dover. Another is the county-wide Kent County Vo-Tech School District. Name the other three school districts.
    a. Smyrna, Appoquinimink, Laurel
    b. Smyrna, Caesar Rodney, Lake Forest
    c. Smyrna, Caesar Rodney, Cape Henlopen
    d. Smyrna, Indian River, Seaford

29. Let's stay with schools for another question. A middle school in the Capital School District in Dover is named after a prominent black physician who encouraged the development of educational opportunities for African Americans. What is the name of the school?
    a. William Henry
    b. Louis L. Redding
    c. Herman M. Holloway, Sr.
    d. Al O. Plant

30. Across the street from Delaware State University is Dover Downs, a horse and car racing track. What type of car races does Dover Downs host?
    a. drag races
    b. classic
    c. Formula 1
    d. stock car

31.   Thanks to no sales tax and city support, Dover is rapidly becoming a shopping mecca. Wal-Mart, one of the largest discount chains in the country, is located in Dover. In what state, whose motto is "The Land of Opportunity," did its colorful founder, Sam Walton, start his first store?
   a.   Arkansas
   b.   California
   c.   North Dakota
   d.   Maine

32.   On Route 13 don't forget to stop at a museum that pays tribute to farm life, past and present, in Delaware. What is the name of this museum?
   a.   Delaware Farm Museum
   b.   Delaware Agricultural Museum
   c.   Delaware Rural Museum
   d.   Delaware Museum of Farm Life

33.   If you drove through Dover on Route 13, you might get the impression that Dover consists only of franchise restaurants and strip malls. To the west of the highway is the downtown area and capital complex--the seat of Delaware's government and the site of many architectural beauties. In what building does the General Assembly meet?
   a.   Kent County Courthouse
   b.   Old State House
   c.   Legislative Hall
   d.   Hall of Records

34.   Also in the capital complex is a square that was the site of many historic events in Delaware, including a 1776 public reading of the Declaration of Independence. What is this square called?
   a.   The Green
   b.   Downtown
   c.   The Square
   d.   Constitution Place

35. In which building are the state's public archives kept?
    a. Delaware Supreme Court
    b. Old Post Office
    c. Hall of Records
    d. Townsend Building

36. In a vault in the archives is the original charter of Charles II's grant of Delaware to whom?
    a. Peter Minuit
    b. James, the Duke of York
    c. William Penn
    d. Lord Baltimore

37. Although the Governor's house may not be the ideal reception center because of its small size, it is a good example of Georgian architecture. What is the name of the Governor's Mansion?
    a. John Dickinson Plantation
    b. Golden Fleece Tavern
    c. Woodburn
    d. The Ridgely House

38. The Governor's Mansion was also a "stop" on the escape route for slaves prior to the Civil War. What is this route called?
    a. Underground Railroad
    b. Freedom Train
    c. Trail of Tears
    d. Wilderness Trail

39. In 1870, the Wilmington Conference Academy was established in Dover. What is the school known as today?
    a. Wesley College
    b. Wilmington College
    c. Burwood Christian Academy
    d. Apple Grove Amish School

40. On the east side of State Street is a 1742 home that was built by a descendent of a Dutchman who helped found New Amsterdam. Name the house.
    a. Hoffecker House
    b. Loockerman House
    c. Cummins House
    d. Lowber House

41. At the corner of Bank and New Streets is the Johnson Victrola Museum, named after Eldridge Reeves Johnson--a Dover resident who invented the Victrola. The Victrola is a trademark for what device?
    a. television
    b. radio
    c. phonograph
    d. camera

42. The oldest Episcopal Church in Kent County is on South State and Water Streets. Name it.
    a. St. James' Church
    b. Friends' Meeting House
    c. Barratt's Chapel
    d. Christ Church

43. Although government activity was transferred from this building to Legislative Hall, the building qualifies as the second oldest capitol in continuous use in the country because it is still used for ceremonial purposes. What building is it?
    a. Old Town Hall
    b. Old Academy
    c. Old Court House
    d. Old State House

44. The Kent County Courthouse (built in 1874) was built on the site of a tavern that is said to have once had a sign with the portrait of King George III. In a fit of patriotism an innkeeper had King George's likeness replaced with an American hero.

Who was the American hero?
a. Thomas Paine
b. George Washington
c. Benjamin Franklin
d. Patrick Henry

45. Lucretia Mott, noted abolitionist and women's rights advocate, spoke on the Court House steps in 1841 and stayed at the Ridgely House directly across on The Green. Mott, along with Elizabeth Cady Stanton, is noted for organizing a women's rights convention in 1848 in New York--the first of its kind. In what city did the convention occur?
a. Seneca Falls   c. Rochester
b. Buffalo   d. Albany

46. In Constitution Park is a four-foot stone cube with the constitution inscribed on it. What rests on top of the cube?
a. a sword
b. a statue of Caesar Rodney
c. a bronze bust of Thomas Jefferson
d. a twelve-foot bronze quill pen

47. Doverites are familiar with the buggies of a community of Amish who live near Dover. The Amish, however, are typically associated with the city of Lancaster. In which state is Lancaster?
a. Ohio
b. Pennsylvania
c. New Jersey
d. Maryland

48. Located in Dover, this company among its many products specializes in dessert products and produces Jell-O. What is the name of this company?
a. Purdue   c. Nature's Pride
b. General Foods   d. Townsend's

49. West of Dover is a one-room schoolhouse built in the first half of the nineteenth century. What is the name of this schoolhouse?
    a. Somerville
    b. Aspendale
    c. Bannister Hall
    d. Octagonal

50. Near the schoolhouse is a road that was mentioned in the best selling book *Blue Highways* (1983) because the author made it a part of his journey around the United States. Delawareans know it as the scenic route. What number is the route?
    a. 9 b. 52 c. 113 d. 40

51. In Dover, Route 13 splits into Route 13 and Route 113. Let's stay on 13, the route that runs toward Seaford. Just outside Dover is Camden. What religious group originally settled Camden?
    a. Baptists
    b. Catholics
    c. Methodists
    d. Quakers

52. South of Dover, the Delaware Railroad runs parallel to Route 13. One of the towns along the railroad is the name of a musical instrument. What is the name of this town?
    a. Horn
    b. Bass
    c. Viola
    d. Bassoon

53. Located near Felton is the only state park in Kent County. What is the name of this state park?
    a. Walter S. Carpenter
    b. Redden State Forest
    c. Lums Pond
    d. Killens Pond

54. Harrington is also along the railroad line and is the site of the Delaware State Fair. The fair features not only farm exhibitions and live entertainment, but also a midway. What is a midway?
    a. rides
    b. a circus
    c. freak show
    d. food

55. Let's return to Dover and take Route 113 south past the Dover Air Force Base toward the beaches. The largest cargo airplane in the world regularly flies into the Dover Air Force Base. What is this airplane called?
    a. 727
    b. DC-8
    c. C-5 Galaxy
    d. B-52

56. The *Shoo Shoo Baby*, a B-17 bomber, is on display in the Dover Air Base Museum. In what war did it play an important role?
    a. World War I
    b. World War II
    c. Vietnam
    d. Persian Gulf

57. During what war was the Dover Air Base established?
    a. World War I
    b. World War II
    c. Korean
    d. Vietnam

58. Just south of the air base is the John Dickinson Mansion, the home of one of Delaware's foremost patriots. The house is near a town whose name is two words. Some sources suggest that the first word is a form of Kidd, one of the pirates that frequented Delaware's shores. The second word means high

41

forested ground surrounded by a marsh. What is the name of this town?
a. Kitts Hummock
b. Kitts Corner
c. Kitts Plateau
d. Kitts Landing

59. The Dickinson Mansion was not built by John, but by his father, a judge, in 1740. What was his father's first name?
a. Thomas
b. George
c. Samuel
d. Caesar

60. Although he was loyal to the Patriot cause and eventually took up arms against the British, John Dickinson did not sign what important document because he felt differences could be worked out?
a. Declaration of Independence
b. Articles of Confederation
c. Constitution
d. Bill of Rights

61. Also near the Dover Air Force Base is the little town of Lebanon, which is on a river that also goes through Dover. What is the name of this river?
a. Nanticoke
b. Mispillion
c. St. Jones
d. Christina

62. A lake in Dover flows into the river mentioned in the last question. What is the name of this lake?
a. Noxontown Lake
b. Silver Lake
c. Haven Lake
d. Garrisons Lake

63. After passing Little Heaven take Route 18 west towards Bowers Beach on the Delaware Bay. North and South Bowers is split by a river that runs through the town. What is the name of this river?
    - a. Brandywine
    - b. St. Jones
    - c. Smyrna
    - d. Murderkill

64. You can take charter boats off Bowers, as well as other Kent County Bay towns, to cast a line for a fish that was given its name because the hook removes easily from its mouth. What is this fish called?
    - a. weakfish
    - b. rainbow trout
    - c. bluefish
    - d. tautog

65. Near Bowers is the site of a prehistoric cemetery and village. What is the name of this site?
    - a. Bay Vista
    - b. Island Field
    - c. Legion
    - d. Barker's Landing

66. Let's get back on Route 113. Just before entering Frederica is a church that is known as the "Cradle of Methodism." What is the name of this colonial church?
    - a. Barratt's Chapel
    - b. Old Drawyer's Church
    - c. Prince George's Chapel
    - d. Christ Church Broad Creek

67. If you had something "Frederica-built" in the nineteenth century, it meant that you had something well-made of good local wood. What were Frederica-built?
    - a. chairs
    - b. rocking horses
    - c. boats
    - d. houses

43

68. Frederica's original name was thought to be too undignified for a Methodist revival. What was the original name?
     a. Burnt House Crossroads
     b. Canterbury Station
     c. Johnny Cake Landing
     d. Flatiron

69. We'll end the Kent journey at North Milford--South Milford is in Sussex County. Milford was known as a shipbuilding town because of its location on a river that provided easy access to the Bay. What is the name of this river?
     a. Indian River
     b. Mispillion
     c. Murderkill
     d. Christina

70. In Milford is an impressive five-bay brick house built by a local religious leader and co-founder of Milford. Name the house.
     a. William Russell House
     b. Jehu Reed House
     c. Parson Thorne House
     d. David Wilson House

Kent County Tour Answers

1. b. Smyrna

2. a. Queen Anne's

3. a. Duck Creek Crossroads

4. a. gambrel

5. b. Commerce

6. c. Clayton

7. b. Conrail

8. d. Kenton and Hartly

9. c. Hartly

10. a. Belmont Hall

11. c. Dutch

12. c. Tri-State Bird Rescue and Research Center

13. a. estuary

14. d. Allee House

15. c. steam boat

16. a. Italy

17. d. Garrisons Lake Golf Club

18. d. Moors

19. b. forest

20. b. muskrat

21. d. Germany

22. c. New Castle

23. a. Charles L. Terry

24. a. James H. Groves

25. b. W. C. Jason

26. d. the General Assembly

27. c. Hornets

28. b. Smyrna, Caesar Rodney, Lake Forest

29. a. William Henry

30. d. stock car

31. a. Arkansas

32. b. Delaware Agricultural Museum

33. c. Legislative Hall

34. a. The Green

35. c. Hall of Records

36. b. James, the Duke of York

37.   c.   Woodburn

38.   a.   Underground Railroad

39.   a.   Wesley College

40.   b.   Loockerman House

41.   c.   phonograph

42.   d.   Christ Church

43.   d.   Old State House

44.   b.   George Washington

45.   a.   Seneca Falls

46.   d.   a twelve-foot bronze quill pen

47.   b.   Pennsylvania

48.   b.   General Foods

49.   d.   Octagonal

50.   a.   9

51.   d.   Quakers

52.   c.   Viola

53.   d.   Killens Pond

54.   a.   rides

55.   c.   C-5 Galaxy

56. b. World War II

57. b. World War II

58. a. Kitts Hummock

59. c. Samuel

60. a. Declaration of Independence

61. c. St. Jones

62. b. Silver Lake

63. d. Murderkill

64. a. weakfish

65. b. Island Field

66. a. Barratt's Chapel

67. c. boats

68. c. Johnny Cake Landing

69. b. Mispillion

70. c. Parson Thorne House

Sussex County Tour

When tourists speed south down Route 13 to Route 1 or cut across Sussex from Washington and Baltimore, they are most likely headed toward the coast of Sussex. There, resort towns, such as Rehoboth and Dewey as well as less developed beaches such as Cape Henlopen State Park, offer the ultimate summer enticements for families: sun, sand, the ocean and, in the case of Rehoboth, a well-traveled boardwalk. Trailing boats, fishermen also come to cast lines in Sussex's waters.

Many residents make a living in Sussex just as their ancestors have done for centuries--working the soil. Like farmers in Kent, Sussex farmers supply food processing industries, provide feed for chickens, and live on farms or in small towns that have remained unchanged for many years. Quaint towns, however, shouldn't belie the fact that Sussex farmers are to be taken seriously--the county ranks number one in the United States in poultry production.

As you might expect, there is the natural pull and tug between longtime residents who view development as an intrusion on their way of life and newcomers who want to benefit from Sussex's traditionally relaxed pace of life. It's not an easy task accommodating both. Sussex Countians and their government have to work to resolve some very basic problems--treating sewage, providing adequate drinking water, and retaining farmland and nature preserves.

For the county's name, Sussex Countians can also thank William Penn, who didn't find the name Deale to his liking. Let's start our journey on Route 1 at the border of Kent and Sussex where you'll find Milford, a town that sits in both counties.

1. Milford dates back to 1787 when Reverend Sydenham Thorne built a grist mill at the ford of the Mispillion River, thus the name Milford. What product did a gristmill produce?
    a. tea
    b. flour
    c. textiles
    d. gun powder

2. One of Delaware's more noted early writers, John Lofland, comes from Milford. He often gets credit for one of Delaware's nicknames--the Diamond State--since he wrote that "Delaware is like a diamond, diminutive, but having within it inherent value." Lofland is often referred to as the Milford Bard. What is a bard?
    a. poet
    b. singer
    c. essayist
    d. artist

3. Delaware's nickname may have also come from one of our first presidents and designer of the University of Virginia who called Delaware "a jewel among the states." Who was he?
    a. George Washington
    b. John Adams
    c. Thomas Jefferson
    d. James Madison

4. When a local dentist began making dental filling materials in his kitchen in 1877, he probably didn't imagine that his nascent business would grow to become one of the largest dental suppliers in the world--the company is still based in Milford. What was the dentist's last name?
    a. Caulk
    b. Stidden
    c. Le Telier
    d. Buckingham

5.	Not far from Milford, a gristmill and pond offer environmental education to the public. What is the name of this historic mill?
	a. Buford Mill
	b. Abbott's Mill
	c. Curtis Mill
	d. Breck's Mill

6.	Just south of Milford is a crossroads town that a New York developer had big plans for when he came to Delaware in the mid-1800s. Although he named the town after a president, his plans for a metropolis never materialized. What president is this town named after?
	a. Madison
	b. Lincoln
	c. Cleveland
	d. Hoover

7.	Due east from Milford on the Delaware Bay, you'll find the only wooden-frame lighthouse in Delaware (no longer in use). Neat what beach area is this lighthouse?
	a. Woodland Beach
	b. Bowers Beach
	c. Slaughter Beach
	d. Rehoboth Beach

8.	A few miles down Route 1 you'll cross the state's longest river. What is it?
	a. Broadkill
	b. Murderkill
	c. Indian River
	d. St. Jones

9.	Two rivers in Delaware end with the suffix *kill*. What does this Dutch suffix mean?
	a. lake
	b. water
	c. shallow
	d. river

10. To the east is Delaware's other national wildlife refuge, a refuge which is noted for being one of the few freshwater marshes on the East Coast. Name the refuge.
    a. Little Creek
    b. Milford Neck
    c. Bombay Hook
    d. Prime Hook

11. To the west a few miles is Milton, a quaint little town that was once a major shipping and ship building center. What is the first name of the famous English poet that Milton is named after?
    a. Robert
    b. John
    c. William
    d. Alfred

12. In the first half of the twentieth century, Milton farmers and their families gathered branches of an evergreen during the winter months to make Christmas wreaths. Their wreaths--made from the state tree--were of such fine quality that Milton wreaths were in demand in other states. What type of holly is the state tree?
    a. American Holly
    b. Chinese Holly
    c. San Jose Holly
    d. English Holly

13. In Milton you'll also find the home of the Draper Company which packs several varieties of vegetables. Under what name are these vegetables sold?
    a. Birdseye
    b. Green Giant
    c. King Cole
    d. Hanover

14. Let's head a few more miles down Route 1 and take Route 9 to Lewes, a beautiful town of historical, architectural, and cultural importance to the state. The Zwaanendael Museum was built in Lewes in 1938 to commemorate Delaware's first, albeit unsuccessful, settlement. The museum was designed to look like the town hall in the city of Hoorn. In what country is Hoorn located?
    a. Germany
    b. England
    c. Holland
    d. Austria

15. If you've walked past the Cannon Ball House on Pilottown Road, you may have tried to pull out the irremovable cannonball imbedded in the brick wall. During what war was the house hit by a cannonball?
    a. French and Indian
    b. Revolutionary
    c. 1812
    d. Civil

16. Also on Pilottown Road is the Maull House where, after John Maull's death, Maull's four sons were raised by his widow and her second husband. Three of the four sons chose a career that is particularly associated with Lewes. What did they become?
    a. river pilots
    b. deep sea fishermen
    c. charter boat captains
    d. farmers

17. Nearby is a remarkable group of privately owned historic homes, each of which was moved to their present location. What is this Lewes block called?
    a. The Green
    b. Shipcarpenter Square
    c. Shipbuilder Square
    d. Commons

18. Further down Pilottown Road is a monument to the Dutchman who, in partnership with others, sent settlers to the ill-fated Zwaanendael settlement. The Dutchman himself arrived a year later to find them all dead. To whom is this monument dedicated?
    a. Jerome Bonaparte
    b. Eric Bjork
    c. David deVries
    d. Peter Stuyvesant

19. On the south side of Kings Highway is the terminus of a railroad that investors built just prior to the turn of the century as part of a commercial link from Baltimore to southern New Jersey. The link included ferries. What is the name of the railroad?
    a. Queen Elizabeth's
    b. Prince George's
    c. King James'
    d. Queen Anne's

20. By boat you can go from Lewes to Rehoboth Bay without entering the Atlantic Ocean. How would you do so?
    a. through the Indian River Inlet
    b. the Lewes and Rehoboth Canal
    c. via Love Creek
    d. across Red Mill Pond

21. The Barcroft Company in Lewes extracts magnesium hydroxide from sea water to be used in the making of what product?
    a. Clairol
    b. Neosporin
    c. Bufferin
    d. Maalox

22. Located on both the bay and ocean is Cape Henlopen State Park. There you'll see tall concrete towers--one of which you can climb. What was the original purpose of these towers?
    a. for radio communications
    b. to serve as lighthouses
    c. to sight enemy submarines
    d. as radar towers

23. Visitors to Cape Henlopen may see signs warning them to keep off the dunes because of potential destruction to the dunes, which are a natural guard against erosion. What specifically could visitors harm on the dunes?
    a. wildlife
    b. dune grass
    c. scrub pines
    d. snakes

24. At a certain time of the year, you may also be warned away from restricted areas because a bird that nests there is rather shy of humans. What bird is this?
    a. sea gull
    b. common terns
    c. piping plover
    d. black skimmer

25. During World War II, Cape Henlopen State Park was a military installation. What branch of the military had a fort there?
    a. Army
    b. Navy
    c. Marines
    d. Air Force

26. All along the Delaware shore you'll see horseshoe crabs. They are misnamed because they are really blue bloods instead of crabs. Instead of iron, what do blue bloods have in their blood?
    a. copper
    b. zinc
    c. magnesium
    d. silver

27. Further south is Rehoboth, Delaware's premier resort area. Its original founders would be amazed to see how much Rehoboth has grown since 1872 when it was founded as a camp meeting site. By what religious sect was it founded?
    a. Protestant
    b. Baptist
    c. Methodist
    d. Catholic

28. Rehoboth is a biblical word meaning what?
    a. meeting camp
    b. sea side
    c. room enough
    d. resort

29. Finish the following: Rehoboth is often referred to as "The Nation's Summer _____."
    a. Fun
    b. Resort
    c. Capital
    d. Sun

30. The Rehoboth Art League--founded in 1938--meets in an unpainted bald-cypress shingled house that is considered a distinctive example of an eighteenth-century Sussex home. Name the house that legend says its owner built to be near pirate treasure buried in the dunes.
    a. Amstel House
    b. The Homestead
    c. Huguenot House
    d. The Hermitage

31. South of Rehoboth is Dewey Beach, a beach many summering
     college students know well. Dewey is named after Admiral
     George Dewey. Dewey was the hero of what battle?
     a. Battle of the Bulge
     b. Battle of Antietam
     c. Battle of the Monitor and Merrimac
     d. Battle of Manila Bay

32. Further south is Delaware Seashore State Park. On what type
     of landform is the park located?
     a. atoll
     b. peninsula
     c. barrier reef
     d. isthmus

33. Passing through the park is the Indian River Inlet which
     empties into the Indian River Bay. What other bay is the inlet
     connected to?
     a. Chesapeake
     b. Little Assawoman
     c. Rehoboth
     d. Delaware

34. What canal connects the Indian River Bay with South Bethany?
     a. Assawoman
     b. Chesapeake and Delaware
     c. Lewes and Rehoboth
     d. Erie

35. Termite damage and the January 1992 northeaster finally
     brought down Chief Little Owl in Bethany, although he was
     eventually rebuilt. What is Chief Little Owl?
     a. billboard
     b. sign
     c. totem-pole
     d. pavilion

36. If it wasn't for a faulty map, Delaware would have even been smaller. Lord Baltimore--who disputed with Penn over territorial claims to the Delmarva peninsula--claimed all territory south of a line drawn due west from Cape Henlopen. Fortunately for Delawareans, his faulty map of the early 1700s showed Cape Henlopen further south. The map was used in a lawsuit he eventually lost. According to this map where was Cape Henlopen thought to be?
    a. Rehoboth
    b. Fenwick Island
    c. Bethany
    d. Dewey

37. Let's head west to Selbyville on Route 54 and then take Route 113 north through some Sussex County small towns. Selbyville was once one of the largest shipping centers for a type of fruit. What was this fruit?
    a. kiwi   c. pears
    b. apples   d. strawberries

38. Delaware's broiler industry, primarily located in Sussex, is one of the most productive in the nation. The demand for chicken feed sustains a booming subsidiary agricultural industry in Delaware. What crops does chicken feed consist of?
    a. cabbage and wheat
    b. corn and soybeans
    c. peas and carrots
    d. apples and peaches

39. West of Selbyville, you'll find the largest freshwater swamp in Delaware, once mined for cypress to make cypress shingles until a great fire in 1930 destroyed the supply. What is the name of this swamp?
    a. Great Pocomoke
    b. Wicomico
    c. Assateague
    d. Prime Hook

40. After pasing through Frankford, you come to a town that is named after General John Dagsworthy, a Delaware patriot who fought in King George's War, the French and Indian War, and the Revolution. Name the town.
    a. Dagschester
    b. Dagston
    c. Dagstown
    d. Dagsboro

41. The next town north on Route 113 is Millsboro, the home of former governor John G. Townsend. When Townsend built this plant in 1957 it was the largest of its kind in the world. What type of plant is it?
    a. vegetable canning
    b. chicken processing
    c. milk pasteurizing
    d. meat packing

42. Millsboro is at the headwaters of what river?
    a. Murderkill
    b. Nanticoke
    c. Indian River
    d. Broadkill

43. Millsboro was originally called Rock Haul or Rock Hole because of the rock fish in the Indian River. Specifically, what type of fish is rock fish?
    a. flounder   c. striped sea bass
    b. blue   d. sword

44. Millsboro is also the site of a Native American powwow that takes place every September and features crafts and dancing. Name the tribe that holds the powwow.
    a. Nanticoke
    b. Lenni Lenape
    c. Minquas
    d. Susquehannock

45. Just north of Millsboro is a state hospital. What is this hospital called?
    a. Stockley Center
    b. Wilmington General
    c. Beebe
    d. Delaware State

46. Next on Route 113 is Georgetown, Sussex County's county seat. Georgetown became the county seat in 1791 because of its more central location in the county. What town was the original county seat in Sussex?
    a. Laurel
    b. Seaford
    c. Harrington
    d. Lewes

47. Georgetown's downtown is unique to all other towns in Delaware. How is the center of town laid out?
    a. as a hexagon
    b. as a circle
    c. as a square
    d. as a triangle

48. In a tradition dating back to colonial times, a celebration is held in Georgetown after state and federal elections to announce the winners of the elections. Even today, winners and losers parade around the town in horse-drawn carriages in a colonial style celebration. What is this day called?
    a. Winner's Circle
    b. Election Day
    c. Delaware Day
    d. Return Day

49. When the Sussex County Court House was completed in 1840, the nationally renowned architect who designed it was dissatisfied with its outside appearance, complaining that the budget didn't enable him to add columns and other decorative elements. Who was this architect?
    a. I. M. Pei
    b. Frank Furness
    c. William Strickland
    d. Frank Lloyd Wright

50. The federal government put people to work during the Depression building a picnic shelter, trails, and dirt roads in Redden State Forest. What New Deal program did they work for?
    a. Works Progress Administration
    b. Civilian Conservation Corps
    c. Housing and Urban Development
    d. Volunteers in Service to America

51. The town of Ellendale sits in Cedar Creek Hundred. A hundred, once used as a political subdivision, no longer serves that purpose. Delaware, which has 32 hundreds, is the only state to retain the term originally brought from England. Sussex has 13 hundreds. Which of the following is not a Sussex hundred?
    a. Duck Creek
    b. Baltimore
    c. Little Creek
    d. Dagsboro

52. About ten miles due west of Ellendale is a small town with a substantial Mennonite community. Name the town that was appropriately named because of a local proliferation of holly.
    a. Greenwood
    b. Wooddale
    c. Woodland
    d. Woodside

SUSSEX COUNTY TOUR

53. Let's leave Route 113 and head west on Route 404 to Bridgeville which is on Route 13. Bridgeville is the home of a nationally known scrapple firm started by two brothers-- Ralph and Paul Adams. What is the name of this firm?
    a. RAPA
    b. Philadelphia
    c. Parks
    d. Jimmy Dean

54. Scrapple is a popular Delmarva breakfast food. What type of meat does scrapple consist of?
    a. chicken
    b. pork
    c. beef
    d. deer

55. Further down Route 13 is Seaford, often referred to as the "Nylon Capital of the World." It was, however, noted in the nineteenth century for the canning of what type of seafood?
    a. clams
    b. crabs
    c. oysters
    d. shrimp

56. The Nanticoke River which flows through Seaford has the distinction of being the only river in the state to flow in which direction?
    a. north   c. east
    b. south   d. west

57. This Seaford mansion was built in the mid-1800s in the Italian Renaissance style. Which governor built the mansion that still goes by his name?
    a. Jehu Davis
    b. Cornelius P. Comegys
    c. William H. Ross
    d. William Burton

63

58. Six governors came from this town that was named for the bushes along Broad Creek. Name the town.
    a. Laurel
    b. Bethel
    c. Greenwood
    d. Blades

59. Don't feel bad about the room you never seem to get around to painting. On Route 24, a few miles east of Laurel, is Old Christ Church. It features a richly hued interior of paneling that has never been painted since the church was built in 1771. What type of wood is it?
    a. oak
    b. pine
    c. spruce
    d. mahogany

60. To see the northern most public stand of cypress trees in North America you have to visit a state park near Laurel. What is the name of this state park?
    a. Redden
    b. Trap Pond
    c. Delaware Seashore
    d. Ellendale

61. To the west of Laurel is Bethel, a quaint town that was once a ship building center and contains so many distinctive ship-carpenter's houses that the entire town is listed on what significant registry?
    a. Who's Who
    b. National Register of Historic Places
    c. Fortune 500
    d. Best Towns

62. What does *Bethel*, a biblical reference, mean?
    a. House of God
    b. Tower of Babel
    c. Temple
    d. Brethren

63. The ship-carpenters of Bethel were noted for building a light open river boat propelled by oars or sails. What kind of boat is it?
    a. clipper ship
    b. row boat
    c. shallop
    d. skiff

64. Near Bethel, you can take a free cable ferry that has crossed the Nanticoke since 1793. What is the name of this ferry?
    a. Martha's Vineyard
    b. Pea Patch Island
    c. Woodland
    d. Cape May-Lewes

65. Since we are at the southern end of the state it's appropriate to ask the state's length. How long is Delaware?
    a. 83 miles
    b. 110 miles
    c. 125 miles
    d. 142 miles

66. What Maryland county would you drive into if you left Sussex heading south on Route 13?
    a. Cecil
    b. Queen Anne's
    c. Talbot
    d. Wicomico

67. We'll end our journey at a town whose motto is "The Little Town Too Big To Be In One State." What is the name of this town?
    a. Delmar
    b. Bridgeville
    c. Selbyville
    d. Millsboro

68. Delmar has a nineteenth-century "Highball Signal." A red ball
     was pulled to the top of a pole as a signal for what to stop?
     a. cars going over a drawbridge
     b. trains
     c. canal boats
     d. cars entering privately owned roads

Sussex County Tour Answers

1. b. flour

2. a. poet

3. c. Thomas Jefferson

4. a. Caulk

5. b. Abbott's Mill

6. b. Lincoln

7. c. Slaughter Beach

8. a. Broadkill

9. d. river

10. d. Prime Hook

11. b. John

12. a. American Holly

13. c. King Cole

14. c. Holland

15. c. 1812

16. a. river pilots

17. b. Shipcarpenter Square

18. c. David deVries

19. d. Queen Anne's

20. b. the Lewes and Rehoboth Canal

21. d. Maalox

22. c. to sight enemy submarines

23. b. dune grass

24. c. piping plover

25. a. Army

26. a. copper

27. c. Methodist

28. c. room enough

29. c. Capital

30. b. The Homestead

31. d. Battle of Manila Bay

32. c. barrier reef

33. c. Rehoboth

34. a. Assawoman

35. c. totem-pole

36. b. Fenwick Island

37. d. strawberries

38. b. corn and soybeans

39. a. Great Pocomoke

40. d. Dagsboro

41. b. chicken processing

42. c. Indian River

43. c. striped sea bass

44. a. Nanticoke

45. a. Stockley Center

46. d. Lewes

47. b. as a circle

48. d. Return Day

49. c. William Strickland

50. b. Civilian Conservation Corps

51. a. Duck Creek

52. a. Greenwood

53. a. RAPA

54. b. pork

55. c. oysters

56. d. west

57. c. William H. Ross

58. a. Laurel

59. b. pine

60. b. Trap Pond

61. b. National Register of Historic Places

62. a. House of God

63. c. shallop

64. c. Woodland

65. b. 110 miles

66. d. Wicomico

67. a. Delmar

68. b. trains

Delaware History

The Colonial Period

Delaware's first settlement was short-lived. In 1631, the Dutch established a settlement near what is now Lewes to hunt whale and trade with the Native Americans. Within a year, a misunderstanding between the Indians and the thirty Dutch settlers led to the settlers' massacre, an incident fortunately not indicative of the way the Delaware Indians, who often proved to be quite helpful, were to treat subsequent settlers.

The Swedes came next and established Fort Christina near present day Wilmington in 1638, although a lack of support from home made New Sweden's twenty-year existence difficult. They were eventually dominated by the Dutch who in turn relinquished control of the area to the English by 1664. Before the Europeans, Delaware Native Americans--the Lenni Lenape in the north and the Nanticoke in the south--thrived in the region by hunting, fishing, and planting such crops as corn, beans, and tobacco. After contact with the Europeans, however, they became consumed with a passion for supplying the Europeans with pelts for barter from a rapidly diminishing supply of beaver.

After Delaware was granted to William Penn in 1683 by the Duke of York, Delaware colonists sent representatives to meet in an assembly with Pennsylvania representatives. Delaware's representatives were an independent-minded and cantankerous crew, however. As the eighteenth century began they agitated for a separate assembly and were finally granted one by a reluctant Penn in 1704. By the time of the Revolutionary War, Delaware was ready to declare independence from England, although many residents supported the English. In 1776 Delaware militia served in every major battle of the war.

We will begin the colonial history trivia with the explorers who first sighted Delaware's shores.

1. Sailing under Dutch employ on his ship the *Half Moon*, the Englishman Henry Hudson discovered the Delaware Bay in 1609. After taking some soundings, Hudson decided that the Delaware Bay would not lead to the route to India he was looking for. What route was Hudson looking for?
    a. around Cape Horn
    b. the Northwest Passage
    c. Panama Canal
    d. Mississippi River

2. Seeking refuge from a storm, English explorer Samuel Argall entered the Delaware Bay in 1610 and named the bay after Thomas West's aristocratic title--Thomas West was the governor of Virginia. What was Thomas West's aristocratic title?
    a. Earl de la Warr
    b. Baron von de la Warr
    c. Prince de la Warr
    d. Lord de la Warr

3. In 1629 Holland granted land at present day Lewes to Samuel Blommaert, Samuel Godyn, and Captain David De Vries. For their land grant they agreed to populate the territory with a specified number of settlers. What title were these three men given?
    a. governors
    b. patroons
    c. patrons
    d. proprietors

4. In 1631, Blommaert, Godyn, and De Vries sent thirty men to establish an ill-fated settlement on Lewes Creek. They named the settlement Zwaanendael. What is the English equivalent of Zwaanendael, a Dutch word?
    a. Valley of the Swans
    b. Beautiful Dale
    c. By the Sea
    d. Swan Song

5.   It's hard to believe now, but these Dutchmen came to hunt for a source of fuel for lamps. What were they hunting for?
   a.   bear
   b.   beaver
   c.   whales
   d.   muskrat

6.   By the 1620s, the Swedish King Gustavus Adolphus became interested in establishing a colony on the Delaware. Although he didn't live to see it, in 1638 a Swedish expedition set sail on two ships--the *Kalmar Nyckel* (*Key of Kalmar*) and the *Fogel Grip* (*Bird Griffin*)--to present day Wilmington. They named their fort and a nearby river after Adolphus's daughter and the new Queen of Sweden. What was her name?
   a.   Elizabeth
   b.   Mispillion
   c.   Brandy
   d.   Christina

7.   The leader of the Swedish expedition was a Dutchman. He had already achieved fame as the governor of the Dutch settlement in New Amsterdam. Who was he?
   a.   John Rising
   b.   Peter Hollander Ridder
   c.   Johan Printz
   d.   Peter Minuit

8.   Many of the settlers on the Swedish expedition were reluctant to come to Delaware. Along with the Swedes were people of another nationality who were often arrested by the Swedes because they illegally burned forest trees in Scandinavia to clear the land for farming--a process known as burn beating. They were given a choice by the Swedes: prison or New Sweden where land clearing was a necessity. Who were these people?
   a.   Finns   c.   Norwegians
   b.   Danes   d.   Estonians

9. According to historian Amandus Johnson, the first African American to settle in Delaware, Black Anthony, was most likely purchased by the Swedes in 1639 and brought to New Sweden where he lived and worked in relative freedom. The first slaves to be brought to America came in 1620. To which settlement were they forced to come?
    a. Massachusetts Bay Colony
    b. Jamestown
    c. Plymouth
    d. New Amsterdam

10. Actually New Sweden wasn't as dangerous as the first settlers thought primarily because the local Indians were peaceful and helpful. Although the Europeans were to eventually refer to them as the Delaware Indians, they are more appropriately called by a name that meant to them the common people or the original people. What is this name?
    a. Lenni Lenape
    b. Minquas
    c. Kickapoo
    d. Choptank

11. The Swedish and Dutch settlers used gifts to purchase land from Lenni-Lenape leaders--Maltahorn is the most noted. What term describes a Lenni-Lenape leader?
    a. Ojibwa
    b. warrior
    c. chief
    d. sachem

12. The Lenni-Lenape spoke a language common to many east coast American natives. What language is it?
    a. Chinookah
    b. Aleut
    c. Algonquian
    d. Siouan

13. The Indians recorded their history on painted sticks referred to as the Walum Olum. They did not, however, use an alphabet. What was on the Walum Olum?
   a. pictures or pictographs
   b. hieroglyphics
   c. totem-pole figures
   d. numbers

14. Native Americans and our early settlers used wampum as a medium of exchange. What is wampum made of?
   a. stone
   b. lobster claws
   c. hard-shell clams
   d. wood

15. We are indebted to the Swedes for the type of houses they built. What were these?
   a. Cape Cod
   b. log houses
   c. huts
   d. saltbox

16. In 1640, the second Swedish expedition arrived with America's first Lutheran preacher, Reorus Torkillus, and the colony's first governor. Who was the first governor?
   a. Peter Hollandaer
   b. Jan Vermeer
   c. Jonker Jan Van derNoot
   d. Desiderius Erasmus

17. The fifth Swedish expedition brought New Sweden's most famous governor, a 400+ pound man who ruled with an iron fist and whom the Indians called "Big Belly." Who was he?
   a. Peter Stuyvesant
   b. William Peter
   c. Johan Printz
   d. Gustavus Adolphus

18. After Big Belly arrived, he moved the seat of government from Fort Christina to an island north of Chester. What is the name of the island?
    a. Honshu
    b. Tinicum
    c. Ellesmere
    d. Baffin

19. Name the Swedish minister who compiled a vocabulary of the language of the Lenni-Lenape in 1646.
    a. Ingrid Bergman
    b. Emmanuel Swedenborg
    c. Johan Campanius
    d. Dag Hammarskjold

20. To control the Delaware River, the Dutch built Fort Casimir directly south of Fort Christina in 1651. Needless to say, the Swedes were upset. Fort Casimir was near the site of what present day Delaware town?
    a. Woodland Beach
    b. New Castle
    c. Lewes
    d. Delaware City

21. Upon his arrival in 1654, a new Swedish governor, Johan Rising, made a fateful decision to take Fort Casimir from the Dutch, an easy task since the fort was garrisoned by only nine Dutch soldiers. Rising changed the name to Fort Trefaldighet--A biblical allusion that refers to *three*. What is the English equivalent of the name?
    a. Fort Tres
    b. Fort Thrice
    c. Fort Triad
    d. Fort Trinity

22.   The Dutch governor in New Amsterdam was incensed over Rising's action and decided to retake Fort Casimir in 1655. Taking no chances, in August 1655 he sent seven ships and over three hundred soldiers to the Delaware River and quickly captured the fort. What was the name of this famous one-legged governor?
a.   Peter Stuyvesant
b.   Alexander D'Hinoyossa
c.   David Pietersen 'de Vries
d.   William Beekman

23.   Fort Casimir, as well as all of New Netherland, was actually owned by The Dutch West India Company. Heavy debt encouraged the company to sell Fort Casimir to the burgomasters of a city in the Netherlands who were interested in reaping profits from Delaware trade. What is the name of this famous city?
a.   Flushing   c.   Amsterdam
b.   Rotterdam   d.   Utrecht

24.   In 1664 the English King Charles II granted land in America--much of it claimed by the Dutch--to his brother. To whom did Charles give the land?
a.   Lord Baltimore
b.   James, the Duke of York
c.   William Penn
d.   Charles I

25.   In 1664, Richard Nicolls, an English commander, captured New Amsterdam from the Dutch and then dispatched two ships to the Delaware River to take New Amstel (formerly Fort Casimir) from the Dutch. Who did Nicolls send to command the two ships?
a.   Robert Carr
b.   William Penn
c.   Alexander d' Hinoyossa
d.   Peter Stuyvesant

26. Apparently not everyone was happy with English rule. Marcus Jacobson was whipped and branded as a troublemaker for spreading rumors that the Swedes were coming to liberate the settlers. Jacobson, who was not Swedish, is nicknamed what?
    a. Canute
    b. the Conquerer
    c. the Terrible
    d. the Long Finn

27. In the 1680s, as payment for a favor owed to the Penn family, Charles II granted the three counties of Pennsylvania to William Penn. Penn, of course, came to America to establish the Quaker faith--a religious sect noted for its industriousness, its rejection of war, and its fair treatment of Native Americans. Historians refer to Penn's attempt to establish his version of a utopian society as what?
    a. Quaker Utopia
    b. Brook Farm
    c. The Holy Experiment
    d. Walden

28. Actually the name Quaker was a rather derogatory name given to the Quakers. What did they call themselves?
    a. Brownists
    b. Baptists
    c. Society of Friends
    d. Methodists

29. Then, as today, Quaker churches are noted for their lack of adornment. What are Quaker churches called?
    a. synagogues
    b. churches
    c. temples
    d. meeting houses

30. Before he even arrived in America, Penn requested and was granted the three counties of Delaware. Why specifically did Penn want Delaware?
    a. for the wetlands
    b. land greed
    c. access to the ocean
    d. for tobacco farming

31. In October of 1682, Penn arrived in America aboard his ship, the *Welcome*, to take possession of his grant. At what town did Penn land?
    a. Dover
    b. Wilmington
    c. Lewes
    d. New Castle

32. For many years, Penn disputed with the proprietor of Maryland over claims to parts of Delaware. Who was the proprietor of Maryland?
    a. Cecil Calvert, Lord Baltimore
    b. John Smith
    c. Lord de la Warr
    d. William Bradford

33. James, the Duke of York, eventually became the King of England. After he was overthrown in 1689, however, Penn's proprietary rights were suspended and Delaware became a royal colony for a couple of years until it was eventually returned to Penn. Who were the new monarchs of England?
    a. Charles and Diana
    b. Henry and Anne
    c. William and Mary
    d. James and Elizabeth

34. Believing it was best that the colonists make some of their own laws, Penn created a representative assembly from both the upper counties (Pennsylvania) and the lower counties (Delaware). The Lower Counties soon started agitating for their own assembly since they, as mostly non-Quakers, had difficulty making joint decisions with the Pennsylvania Quakers, who, in particular, refused to raise money for a militia to protect the Delaware coast from pirates. By 1704 Penn granted Delaware its own assembly. Where did it meet?
    a. Dover
    b. Wilmington
    c. Newark
    d. New Castle

35. Delaware colonists were no strangers to pirates who often plundered towns and farms in lower Delaware in the late 1700s and early 1800s. One famous pirate was Captain Blackbeard who was also known as Bluebeard. Name the other well-known pirate who sailed Delaware waters.
    a. Kidd
    b. Hook
    c. Canoot
    d. Avery

36. Which of the following terms describe pirates who are legally sanctioned by a country to attack ships of an enemy country?
    a. scalawags   c. blackguard
    b. knaves   d. privateers

37. Delaware colonists, as did other colonists, paid the way for immigrants who agreed to work as servants for a few years to repay the debt. What were these servants known as?
    a. man servants
    b. indentured servants
    c. slaves
    d. housekeepers

38. In 1701, Penn granted this religious group from Wales a track of land near Iron Hill where they could mine iron ore, farm, and practice their religious beliefs. What religion did they practice?
   a. Methodist
   b. Welsh Baptist
   c. Protestant
   d. Catholic

39. Name the painter who arrived in Wilmington with his pastor brother in 1711 and went on to distinguish himself as one of our great early painters.
   a. Gustavus Hesselius
   b. Johan T. Sergel
   c. Anders Zorn
   d. Carl Milles

40. In 1731 Thomas Willing founded Wilmington and named the town Willington. The name was changed to Wilmington--after the Earl of Wilmington, Spenser Compton--when Penn gave the town a charter in 1739. The town really took off as a market and shipping center when this Quaker merchant and his wife moved there in 1735. What is the merchant's name?
   a. George Fox
   b. Thomas McKean
   c. Thomas Garrett
   d. William Shipley

41. The same year that Wilmington received a charter, Anglican clergyman George Whitefield landed at Lewes and began preaching the gospel. His speeches throughout the colonies drew thousands and were noted for their religious fervor. Whitefield was part of a revivalist movement in America known as what?
   a. the Rebirth
   b. the Great Revival
   c. the Great Awakening
   d. Sinners Beware

42. In 1742, Oliver Canby built the first large scale mill of its kind on the Brandywine River producing a product that Wilmington was to be noted for. What type of mill was Canby's?
a. corn
b. paper
c. textiles
d. flour

43. Throughout the 1700s, the English vied with another nation for control of North America. This resulted in a war that took place on American soil during the years 1756 - 1763. The Delaware militia was sent to fight in this war. Name the war.
a. The French and Indian War
b. King Phillip's War
c. Revolutionary War
d. Civil War

44. In 1761, James Adams established the first printing press in Delaware and printed its first newspaper--the *Wilmington Courant*--a year later. Name the famous non-Delawarean who supplied much of Delaware's printing needs before Adams.
a. Johann Gutenberg
b. Benjamin Franklin
c. William Caxton
d. Robert Hoe

45. Seventy years after the land disputes first started, the Lord Chancellor of England finally settled the boundary disputes between the Calvert family and the Penn family. From 1763 - 1768 these two famous surveyors surveyed the southern and western boundaries of Delaware. Who were they?
a. George Washington and Thomas Jefferson
b. Charles Mason and Jeremiah Dixon
c. Merriwether Lewis and William Clark
d. William and John Penn

46. Of the two delegates that Delaware sent to the Stamp Act Congress in 1765 to protest British taxation, one was New Castle County lawyer Thomas McKean. Who was the other representative who was to play such an influential role in Delaware history?
   a. Caesar Rodney
   b. George Read
   c. Gunning Bedford
   d. John Dickinson

47. In 1775, Delaware sent three delegates to the Second Continental Congress in Philadelphia. Two were Caesar Rodney and Thomas McKean. Who was the third?
   a. Jehu Davis
   b. Peter Minuit
   c. William Markham
   d. George Read

48. Rodney was in Dover on pressing business when the Congress decided to cast the vote for independence. Rodney made his famous ride to cast Delaware's vote for independence since the Delaware delegation's vote was split. With or without Delaware, the Congress could still have declared independence. Why?
   a. Delaware wasn't considered important.
   b. Delaware was too small.
   c. They already had a majority of nine votes.
   d. Sentiment was too strong for a separation.

49. On June 15, 1776, the Delaware assembly met in New Castle and voted to declare independence from England. We still honor that day every year. What is that day called?
   a. Independence Day
   b. Armistice Day
   c. Separation Day
   d. Veteran's Day

50. After declaring independence, Delaware and the rest of the colonies prepared to fight the British. The Delaware regiment must have looked quite impressive in their blue coats and tan pants. The words that were written on their black leather hats are on the state seal and the flag today. What are these words?
   a. The First State
   b. Live Free or Die
   c. Blue Hens
   d. Liberty and Independence

51. The Delaware General Assembly authorized a convention of ten members from each county to write Delaware's first constitution. The new constitution created a bicameral assembly and changed the name of Delaware officially from the "Counties of New Castle, Kent and Sussex upon Delaware" to Delaware State. The constitution was completed by September of what year?
   a. 1765   c. 1812
   b. 1776   d. 1861

52. The constitution of 1776 did not ban slavery, but it did decrease the likelihood that more slaves would be brought into the state. With reference to slavery, what did the constitution ban?
   a. importing slaves into the state
   b. selling them
   c. interracial marriage
   d. owning slaves

53. Started in 1776, and put into effect in 1781, the Articles of Confederation served as our country's first constitution until our present constitution was completed in 1787. What famous Delawarean wrote the first draft of the Articles of Confederation?
   a. Thomas McKean   c. George Read
   b. Gunning Bedford   d. John Dickinson

54. After British troops under General Howe landed at the head of the Elk River in the late summer of 1777, they marched toward Akientown (now Glasgow) and skirmished with a contingent of Washington's men at Cooch's Bridge, the only Revolutionary War fight on Delaware soil. Howe's troops then turned toward Chadds Ford, Pennsylvania, where they defeated Washington and his troops on September 11, 1777. What is this battle called?
    a. Lexington and Concord
    b. The Battle of Yorktown
    c. The Battle of the Brandywine
    d. The Battle of Cowpens

55. Delaware's state bird, the Blue Hen Chicken, dates back to the Revolutionary War period when Delaware soldiers used to carry the roosters of the blue hen breed with them. What did they use the roosters for?
    a. singing
    b. cock fights
    c. racing
    d. company

56. Not all Delawareans were sympathetic to the Patriot cause. Delaware's most notorious Tory lived in Kent County and was accused of harassing local patriots. His refusal to take an oath of allegiance led to a shootout with a posse sent to arrest him. The death of one of the deputies eventually led to his hanging in 1788--much to the dismay of the notable patriot Caesar Rodney who hoped that the governor would pardon the Tory and former British Army officer. Who was he?
    a. Edward Braddock
    b. Cheney Clow
    c. Henry Clinton
    d. John Burgoyne

57. What year did the Revolutionary War end?
    a. 1780   c. 1785
    b. 1783   d. 1787

58. Organized in 1788, Delaware's first abolition society included Camden founder Warner Mifflin. What religious group formed the society?
    a. Catholics
    b. Methodists
    c. Protestants
    d. Quakers

59. Five Delaware delegates attended the Constitutional Convention in Philadelphia in 1787. Four of them were Richard Bassett, Gunning Bedford, Jr., Jacob Broom, and George Reed. The fifth was noted for his active support of small states' rights. Who was he?
    a. John Dickinson
    b. John McKinley
    c. Louis McLane
    d. John Clayton

60. Delaware was the first state to ratify the Constitution. On what date did delegates meet at Battell's Tavern in Dover to ratify the Constitution?
    a. July 4, 1776
    b. December 7, 1787
    c. January 1, 1802
    d. April 6, 1813

61. In 1792, Delaware adopted its second constitution. One of the changes from the first constitution was to add a court of equity, or fairness, that is still in existence today. Delaware, in fact, is one of a few states to have such a court. What is it called?
    a. Supreme Court   c. Family Court
    b. Court of Chancery   d. Superior Court

62. Delaware's first bank was chartered in 1795. Name this bank.
    a. Bank of Delaware
    b. Mellon Bank
    c. Wilmington Trust
    d. Marine Midland

63. In 1795, who started the first cotton mill in the state?
    a. Thomas Gilpin
    b. Caesar A. Rodney
    c. Jacob Broom
    d. Samuel Harlan

64. In 1796, the General Assembly passed a law that created a fund of money derived from marriage and tavern licenses. What was the fund created for?
    a. public schools
    b. orphans
    c. road building
    d. senior citizens

65. Legend had it that this English privateer was loaded with treasure when it sank off Cape Henlopen during a storm in 1798. To the disappointment of many Delawareans, the claims proved unfounded when the ship was raised in 1986. What is the name of this ship?
    a. *Half Moon*
    b. *Kalmer Nyckel*
    c. *Discovery*
    d. *Debraak*

The Colonial Period Answers

1. b. the Northwest Passage

2. d. Lord de la Warr

3. b. patroons

4. a. Valley of the Swans

5. c. Whales. Their ship, in fact, was named the *Whale*.

6. d. Christina

7. d. Peter Minuit

8. a. Finns

9. b. Jamestown

10. a. Lenni Lenape

11. d. sachem

12. c. Algonquian

13. a. pictures or pictographs

14. c. hard-shell clams

15. b. log houses

16. a. Peter Hollandaer

17. c. Johan Printz

18. b. Tinicum

19. c. Johan Campanius

20. b. New Castle

21. d. Fort Trinity

22. a. Peter Stuyvesant

23. c. Amsterdam

24. b. James, the Duke of York

25. a. Robert Carr

26. d. the Long Finn

27. c. The Holy Experiment

28. c. Society of Friends

29. d. meeting houses

30. c. access to the ocean

31. d. New Castle

32. a. Cecil Calvert, Lord Baltimore

33. c. William and Mary

34. d. New Castle

35. a. Kidd

36. d. privateers

37. b. indentured servants

38. b. Welsh Baptist

39. a. Gustavus Hesselius

40. d. William Shipley

41. c. the Great Awakening

42. d. flour

43. a. The French and Indian War

44. b. Benjamin Franklin

45. b. Charles Mason and Jeremiah Dixon

46. a. Caesar Rodney

47. d. George Read

48. c. They already had a majority of nine votes.

49. c. Separation Day

50. d. Liberty and Independence

51. b. 1776

52. a. importing slaves into the state

53. d. John Dickinson

54. c. The Battle of the Brandywine

55. b. cock fights

56. b. Cheney Clow

57. b. 1783

58. d. Quakers

59. a. John Dickinson

60. b. December 7, 1787

61. b. Court of Chancery

62. a. Bank of Delaware

63. c. Jacob Broom

64. a. public schools

65. d. *Debraak*

The Nineteenth Century

As the nineteenth century began, the picturesque and powerful Brandywine River continued to play an important role in Delaware's history. Convinced he had found one of the best rivers in the country for turning millstones, the emigrant Frenchman, E. I. du Pont, chose the Brandywine as the site for his gunpowder works. Other industries--including flour, textile, and paper mills--flourished along the Brandywine making the most of the river's power and access to the Bay. As a consequence of industrial development in New Castle County, Wilmington grew to become the state's urban center and the site of such industries as shipbuilding and railroad car-making-- industries for which the city was to achieve national recognition.

Downstate, lack of easy access to urban markets stifled farmers for the first half of the century. However, the completion of the Delaware Railroad south to the Maryland border in 1859 changed the fortunes of many downstate farmers who began to practice more progressive farming techniques and who were able to transport their crops to city markets from the new towns that sprang up along the rail line. Along Delaware's southern rivers, shipyards built sailing ships of all sizes and spurred the growth of such towns as Milford, Frederica, and Bethel.

Although Delaware's slave population had been declining since 1790, Delaware was still officially a slave state on the eve of the Civil War. Unionists outnumbered and outvoted southern sympathizers and Delaware remained in the Union, fortuitously avoiding Union Army occupation. No Civil War battles were fought on Delaware soil, although the Delaware Regiment--led at first by Robert Lockwood--did distinguish itself in all the major battles. After the war the state turned its thoughts toward industrial and economic growth as well as improving a weak public education system.

Let's begin this century with a du Pont.

1. In 1802, E. I. du Pont founded a dynasty when he built a gunpowder mill along the Brandywine. He knew his business well for he had studied with a famous French chemist. Who was this chemist?
   a. Albert Einstein
   b. Robert Wilhelm Bunsen
   c. Antoine Lavoisier
   d. Marie Curie

2. In January of 1803, Vice-President Aaron Burr was forced to lengthen his visit to Wilmington because of the heavy snow. Over a year later, Burr would kill the country's first Secretary of the Treasury in a duel. What famous American did Burr kill?
   a. Alexander Hamilton
   b. Henry Knox
   c. Edmund Randolph
   d. Thomas Jefferson

3. On July 25, 1805, thousands of people gathered near Smyrna to attend the first camp meeting of a religious denomination that was to become important in Delaware history. What was this denomination?
   a. Baptist
   b. Protestant
   c. Methodist
   d. Catholic

4. After Robert Fulton invented the first commercially successful steamboat in 1807, steamboats soon became a common sight on the Delaware Bay and River ferrying cargo and passengers to and from Delaware coastal towns. What was the name of Fulton's steamboat?
   a. *Clermont*
   b. *Turbinia*
   c. *Polacca*
   d. *Phoenix*

5. Delaware's official state bank started in 1807. What was the name of this bank?
    a. Bank of Delaware
    b. Wilmington Trust
    c. Farmers Bank
    d. Baltimore Trust

6. Well-kept toll roads were important back in the days when long distance travel could be difficult. The first toll road in Delaware was authorized in 1808, and although it's no longer a toll road, it still goes by the same name. What was the name of this former turnpike?
    a. Newport and Gap Pike
    b. Route 13
    c. I-95
    d. Kirkwood Highway

7. By 1810, Delaware's population was over 72,000. During what year was the country's first census taken?
    a. 1770
    b. 1780
    c. 1790
    d. 1800

8. It's hard to believe but Delaware once had two United States Representatives. After the 1810 census Delaware was allocated two Representatives chosen at large. After what census did Delaware lose a Representative?
    a. 1820
    b. 1830
    c. 1840
    d. 1850

9. Because African Americans were generally accepted by Delaware Methodists, many blacks joined the Methodist Church. In 1805, however, dissatisfied with segregated seating in the Asbury Methodist Church in Wilmington, local blacks started their own church. In 1812, blacks further separated themselves from white Methodist control by forming their own conference, whose mother church was the African Methodist Church. What African-American preacher led the movement to start an independent black conference?
    a. Absalom Jones
    b. Alice Dunbar-Nelson
    c. Peter Spenser
    d. W. C. Jason

10. After the independent black conference was formed, African-American Methodists from the region started meeting in Wilmington each August to celebrate the birth of their conference. The celebration which was revived in the 1980s is still being held. What is the name of this celebration?
    a. Martin Luther King Day
    b. Kwanza
    c. Black Saturday
    d. Big Quarterly

11. Many Delawareans fought in the War of 1812. Two famous seamen were, in fact, from Delaware. Captain Jacob Jones, from Smyrna, thrilled the public when he captured the British Ship, the *Frolic*, in the West Indies after a fierce battle. As the commander of an American fleet, Commodore Thomas Macdonough, from St. Georges, won a decisive naval battle against the British. On what famous body of water did this battle occur?
    a. Lake Michigan
    b. Lake Erie
    c. Lake Champlain
    d. Lake Superior

12. No one was killed during an unsuccessful bombardment of a Delaware town by a British fleet during the War of 1812. A local poetaster best described the effort: "The commander and all his men/Shot a dog and killed a hen." Where in Delaware did the bombardment occur on April 6, 1813?
   a. New Castle
   b. Kitts Hummock
   c. Lewes
   d. Fenwick Island

13. In 1816, the first Catholic church in Delaware was founded in Wilmington and named after the first pope. What is the name of this church?
   a. St. Peter's
   b. St. Elizabeth's
   c. St. Joseph's
   d. St. James'

14. Census reports from 1790 to the Civil War suggest that Delaware slave owners were gradually emancipating their slaves in spite of the fact that Delaware legislatures refused to pass abolition laws. The rights of free blacks, however, were severely limited by statutes. What term describes the process of freeing slaves?
   a. to enfranchise
   b. to set free
   c. to release
   d. to manumit

15. A Delaware first is machine-made paper. Who first manufactured paper on a cylinder in his Brandywine mill in 1817?
   a. Thomas Gilpin
   b. Ann Parish
   c. Edward Cooch
   d. H. Fletcher Brown

16. During the 1820s, Delaware's most notorious kidnapper captured free blacks and sent them to the South for profit via the Nanticoke River and the Chesapeake Bay. In 1824, she was finally jailed for murder when human remains were uncovered near her house. Who was she?
     a. Patty Gunn
     b. Patty Cannon
     c. Patty Bullet
     d. Patty Axe

17. In 1824, Washington's war comrade and friend to the du Ponts visited Wilmington. Name the Frenchman.
     a. Marquis de Lafayette
     b. Charles DeGaulle
     c. Guy Mollet
     d. Charles de Talleyrand

18. The Chesapeake and Delaware Canal was completed in 1829, after five years of construction by a private corporation. Who now owns and operates the C and D Canal?
     a. Congress
     b. U.S. Army Corps of Engineers
     c. Navy Seals
     d. State of Delaware

19. A new town, Delaware City, was created at the canal's terminus in the Delaware Bay. The town's promoters were so thrilled at the city's commercial potential that they named the main street after the governor of New York who was instrumental in developing the Erie Canal. Who was this governor?
     a. DeWitt Clinton
     b. Alfred E. Smith
     c. Franklin D. Roosevelt
     d. Herbert H. Lehman

20. Shipbuilding yards sprang up in towns along southern Delaware rivers because of, in part, a plentiful supply of local wood. What type of wood was predominately used to build the wooden sailing ships in southern Delaware?
    a. teak
    b. mahogany
    c. pine
    d. oak

21. The School Law of 1829 set up local public school districts and provided small matching grants to support them. In what state were public school laws first enacted?
    a. Vermont
    b. Pennsylvania
    c. Massachusetts
    d. Georgia

22. In 1831, the first railroad track was opened in Delaware using horse-drawn cars. Between which cities in Delaware and Maryland was it opened?
    a. New Castle and Frenchtown
    b. Wilmington and Elkton
    c. Newark and Rising Sun
    d. Dover and Chestertown

23. The year 1831 saw the beginnings of the commercial planting of a fruit that was to make many farmers wealthy until the crop was ruined by disease. What is this fruit?
    a. apples
    b. pears
    c. coconuts
    d. peaches

24. In 1831, primarily due to the spread of malicious rumors, white Delawareans, particularly in southern Delaware, were afraid of mass slave uprisings. This fear was due to what slave rebellion that had taken place in Virginia the same year?
   a. Idi Amin's Rebellion
   b. John Brown's Rebellion
   c. Nat Turner's Rebellion
   d. Toussaint L'Ouverture's Rebellion

25. In 1831, Delaware adopted its third constitution. Instead of annually, this constitution stipulated that elections be held how often?
   a. every two years   c. every four years
   b. every three years   d. every six years

26. In 1833, a college that was eventually to become the University of Delaware was chartered. What was its name?
   a. Wilmington College
   b. Newark College
   c. Wesley College
   d. Goldey Beacom College

27. On February 11, 1835, the General Assembly authorized the raising of money for school and state expenses, although the money wasn't raised by taxes. How was this money raised?
   a. gambling
   b. sale of state lands
   c. tariffs
   d. lottery

28. What large scale public project was completed in 1835 in Lewes so that the harbor would provide a haven for ships during storms?
   a. Wilmington Marine Terminal
   b. Indian River Inlet
   c. Delaware Breakwater
   d. Chesapeake and Delaware Canal

29.   In the first half of the eighteenth century, factories that produced world-class railroad cars, carriages, and ships started along the Christina River. What company along the Christina produced the *Bangor*--the world's first seagoing cast iron steamer?
   a.   DuPont
   b.   Bancroft
   c.   Pusey and Jones
   d.   Harlan and Hollingsworth

30.   In 1838, the P. W. and B. Railroad was completed across northern Delaware. What does P. W. and B. stand for?
   a.   Philadelphia, Wilmington, and Baltimore
   b.   Pittsburg, Wilmington, and Bridgeton
   c.   Paoli, Wyoming, and Bridgeville
   d.   Pennsylvania, Washington, and Boston

31.   Renowned orator and statesman Daniel Webster spoke in Wilmington in 1840.   Which state did Senator Webster represent?
   a.   Vermont
   b.   Massachusetts
   c.   Pennsylvania
   d.   Kentucky

32.   In March of 1841, the famous author of *The Tale of Two Cities* visited Wilmington. Who was he?
   a.   Charles Dickens
   b.   Thomas Hardy
   c.   E. M. Forester
   d.   Joseph Conrad

33.   In 1847, troops were recruited in Delaware for what war?
   a.   Spanish-American
   b.   Mexican
   c.   Civil War
   d.   French and Indian

34. In 1850, as secretary of state for the federal government, Delawarean John M. Clayton negotiated the Clayton-Bulwer Treaty with Great Britain which agreed to joint control over a potential canal across the Isthmus of Panama. Which president did Clayton serve?
     a. Martin Van Buren
     b. Zachary Taylor
     c. James K. Polk
     d. James Buchanan

35. Kent and Sussex County farmers were at a disadvantage to New Castle County farmers by the 1850s since New Castle County farmers had ready access to market by railroad transportation. Consequently, another railroad, the Delaware Railroad, was started in Wilmington and built south along the western side of the state. Why did the railroad engineers choose the western part of the state rather than east along the coast?
     a. It's closer to Maryland.
     b. Political bribes encouraged them.
     c. It's a more direct route.
     d. It's too marshy along the eastern part.

36. Slave ownership was still officially sanctioned in Delaware on the eve of the Civil War, although many Delawareans had turned against it. Delawareans, as well as the rest of the country, were made keenly aware of the depredations of slavery when *Uncle Tom's Cabin* was published in 1852. Who wrote it?
     a. Nathaniel Hawthorne
     b. Emily Dickinson
     c. Harriet Beecher Stowe
     d. Henry David Thoreau

37. Oysters were a livelihood for these bay town residents who held "Big Thursday" in August to celebrate the opening of the season. The tradition dates back to 1852. Name the town where these celebrations occurred.
    a. Dewey
    b. Rehoboth
    c. Bowers Beach
    d. Slaughter Beach

38. It didn't take long for this Dover canning company (founded 1855) to achieve national recognition for its canned chicken and fruits. Name it.
    a. Pusey and Jones
    b. Switt, Courtney, and Beecher
    c. Harlan and Hollingsworth
    d. Richardson and Robbins

39. Delaware tried to adopt a fourth constitution in 1853, but after being submitted to popular vote it was rejected. What term describes the process of allowing the public to decide important issues?
    a. referendum
    b. initiative
    c. popular vote
    d. electoral college

40. Delaware State University wasn't the first African-American college in the region. Name the Oxford, Pennsylvania, college which opened in 1856, and was established for the "scientific, classical, and theological education of black males."
    a. Cheyney
    b. Lincoln
    c. Tuskegee
    d. Morgan

41. In 1856, the Delaware Railroad was finally completed at this southern Delaware border town. Name the town.
    a. Dagsboro
    b. Laurel
    c. Delmar
    d. Fenwick Island

42. On the eve of the Civil War, what was the approximate population of Delaware?
    a. 56,000
    b. 112,000
    c. 243,000
    d. 870,000

43. Delaware stayed with the Union during the Civil War in spite of some sympathy for the Confederate cause, particularly in southern Delaware. What did Maryland do?
    a. stayed with the Union
    b. went with the Confederacy

44. To stave off a widening of the rebellion, in 1861 Lincoln proposed the idea of paying slave owners to free their slaves. Lincoln decided to test the idea in Delaware because of its size and border state status. The proposal was defeated before it even reached the floor of the General Assembly after a polling of Delaware assemblymen revealed a lack of support. What was this plan called?
    a. compensated emancipation
    b. Missouri Compromise
    c. abolition
    d. Kansas-Nebraska Bill

45. Although some Delawareans had mixed feelings about which side to support during the Civil War, the editor of the *Georgetown Messenger* made clear his choice. Was the paper pro-Union or pro-Confederacy?
    a. pro-Union
    b. pro-Confederacy

46. Delaware's first volunteer regiment suffered heavy losses near Sharpsburg in Maryland when General Lee attempted his first invasion of the North. What is the name of this famous battle?
    a. Vicksburg
    b. Gettysburg
    c. Bull Run
    d. Antietam

47. In January of 1863, Lincoln issued the Emancipation Proclamation to free slaves. The proclamation did not, however, have any legal effect in Delaware where slaves retained their status until the end of the war. Why didn't the proclamation technically free slaves in Delaware?
    a. The proclamation applied only to Confederate states.
    b. The General Assembly voted against it.

48. Close to a thousand Delaware African Americans volunteered for enlistment during the Civil War. What renowned black regiment from Massachusetts did the 1989 movie *Glory* portray?
    a. 54th   c. 18th
    b. 31st   d. 9th

49. In the election of 1864, President Lincoln did not carry Delaware's three electoral votes. Who did?
    a. Franklin Pierce
    b. Grover Cleveland
    c. John C. Breckinridge
    d. Ulysses S. Grant

50. In April of 1865, Brigadier General Thomas A. Smyth, an Irish immigrant and Delawarean, was killed while in pursuit of General Lee and his troops. Lee was headed to the town where he would finally surrender. What is the name of this town?
    a. Savannah   c. Appomattox
    b. Atlanta   d. Charleston

51. Many women must have been pleased when a special convention--the first of its kind--was held in Wilmington in 1869. What was its name?
    a. suffrage
    b. voting
    c. minority rights
    d. education

52. The Fifteenth Amendment was ratified in 1870, although Delaware did not vote in favor of it. The Fifteenth Amendment extended African Americans the right to do what?
    a. to live in freedom
    b. to vote
    c. to live where they pleased
    d. to own property

53. The first building of this former Wilmington high school for black students was built in 1869. What was the name of the school?
    a. Jason   c. Redding
    b. DuBois   d. Howard

54. What religious denomination founded Wesley College in Dover in 1873?
    a. Lutheran
    b. Baptist
    c. Methodist
    d. Presbyterian

55. Started in 1876, Wilmington's first morning newspaper, the *Morning Herald*, became the long-lasting *Wilmington Morning News* four years later. Which evening paper did the *Morning News* merge with in the 1980s to become the *News Journal?*
    a. *Evening Journal*
    b. *Federal Ark*
    c. *The Blue Hen's Chicken*
    d. *Mercury*

56. Name the woman who became the first African-American principal of Howard High School in 1876.
    a. Edwina B. Kruse
    b. Mary McLeod Bethune
    c. Sharon Pratt Dixon
    d. Toni Morrison

57. Although a few Jews had been in Delaware since colonial times, it wasn't until 1881 that about fifteen Jews met in Wilmington to hold the first formal religious service to celebrate the Jewish New Year. What Hebraic term describes the Jewish New Year?
    a. Passover
    b. Rosh Hashanah
    c. Chanukah
    d. Yom Kippur

58. By 1883, ex-convicts no longer had to wear what item that publicly marked them as ex-convicts?
    a. badge
    b. jacket
    c. tattoo
    d. ball and chain

59. In 1887, this farmers' organization sued the Pennsylvania Railroad--the owners of the Delaware Railroad--charging them with unfair shipping prices. What was the name of this farmers' organization?
    a. Agriculture Commission
    b. Delaware State Grange
    c. Silk Committee
    d. Agriculture Society

60. In 1889, this form of punishment was outlawed for women, although it lasted as a punishment for men well into the twentieth century. What was it?
    a. whipping post
    b. execution
    c. life imprisonment
    d. solitary confinement

61. This southern Delaware border town almost burned to the ground when fire enveloped it in 1891. What is the name of this town?
    a. Millsboro
    b. Selbyville
    c. Delmar
    d. Blades

62. Delaware State College (now Delaware State University) was founded in 1891, as an all black land-grant college. As a college of "Agriculture and Mechanic Arts" it qualified to receive a share of the funds appropriated from the sale of federal land. Name the senator from Vermont who was primarily responsible for the federal land-grant act.
    a. Douglas
    b. Morrill
    c. Webster
    d. Clay

63. In 1895 the General Assembly adopted the state flower. What is the Delaware state flower?
    a. mountain laurel
    b. clover
    c. rhododendron
    d. peach blossom

64. Delaware's present constitution was written in 1897. How many constitutions had been written and ratified before the constitution of 1897?
    a. one
    b. three
    c. five
    d. eight

65. Unfortunately, the constitution of 1897 did not enfranchise women in spite of intensive lobbying by suffragists. Women property owners, however, did have the right to vote in what elections?
    a. federal
    b. county
    c. local town
    d. school board

66. Single-taxers also lobbied unsuccessfully to have their views of taxation incorporated into the constitution. What is the single tax a tax on?
    a. land, but not improvements
    b. income
    c. products
    d. families

67. Segregated schools for blacks and whites were the norm in the nineteenth century, with black schools being woefully underfunded. A United States Supreme Court decision in 1896 affirmed school segregation by declaring that "separate but equal" facilities were constitutional. What is the name of this Supreme Court decision?
    a. *Gitlow v. New York*
    b. *Engel v. Vitale*
    c. *Plessy v. Ferguson*
    d. *Marbury v. Madison*

68. At the end of the nineteenth century and into the twentieth, John Edward Addicks, who made his fortune with gas companies, moved to Delaware and tried to buy his way into elective office. What office did Addicks seek?
    a. U.S. Senator
    b. U.S. Representative
    c. State Senator
    d. Governor

The Nineteenth Century Answers

1. c. Antoine Lavoisier

2. a. Alexander Hamilton

3. c. Methodist

4. a. *Clermont*

5. c. Farmers Bank

6. a. Newport and Gap Pike

7. c. 1790

8. a. 1820

9. c. Peter Spenser

10. d. Big Quarterly

11. c. Lake Champlain

12. c. Lewes

13. a. St. Peter's

14. d. to manumit

15. a. Thomas Gilpin

16. b. Patty Cannon

17. a. Marquis de Lafayette

18. b. U.S. Army Corps of Engineers

19.   a.   DeWitt Clinton

20.   d.   oak

21.   c.   Massachusetts

22.   a.   New Castle and Frenchtown

23.   d.   peaches

24.   c.   Nat Turner's Rebellion

25.   a.   every two years

26.   b.   Newark College

27.   d.   lottery

28.   c.   Delaware Breakwater

29.   d.   Harlan and Hollingsworth

30.   a.   Philadelphia, Wilmington, and Baltimore

31.   b.   Massachusetts

32.   a.   Charles Dickens

33.   b.   Mexican

34.   b.   Zachary Taylor

35.   d.   It's too marshy along the eastern part.

36.   c.   Harriet Beecher Stowe

37.   c.   Bowers Beach

38. d. Richardson and Robbins

39. a. referendum

40. b. Lincoln

41. c. Delmar

42. b. 112,000

43. a. stayed with the Union

44. a. compensated emancipation

45. a. pro-Union

46. d. Antietam

47. a. The proclamation applied only to Confederate states.

48. a. 54th

49. c. John C. Breckinridge

50. c. Appomattox

51. a. suffrage

52. b. to vote

53. d. Howard

54. c. Methodist

55. a. *Evening Journal*

56. a. Edwina B. Kruse

57.   b.   Rosh Hashanah

58.   b.   jacket

59.   b.   Delaware State Grange

60.   a.   whipping post

61.   c.   Delmar

62.   b.   Morrill

63.   d.   peach blossom

64.   b.   three

65.   d.   school board

66.   a.   land, but not improvements

67.   c.   *Plessy v. Ferguson*

68.   a.   U.S. Senator

The Twentieth Century

It is a twentieth century phenomenon that for many out-of-staters Delaware is synonymous with DuPont. Although DuPont began in 1802 and was the largest gunpowder company in the United States by the end of the century, it wasn't until three du Pont cousins--Pierre, Coleman, and Alfred--took control of the company in 1902, and expanded into chemicals that the company grew to achieve national and international fame. Downstate, an agricultural revolution was about to take place. When Delaware's broiler industry began just prior to World War II, few could have imagined just how important an industry it would become for Sussex Countians.

After World War II, Delaware African Americans began a concerted effort to challenge long accepted segregation practices in schools and public facilities. In 1952 a desegregation case was successfully argued before the Delaware Chancery Court thus allowing two young black girls to attend Claymont High School--a case that was to become in 1954 part of the famous Brown v. the Board of Education of Topeka, Kansas. *The State School Board was reluctant to move too quickly, however, and it wasn't until 1966 that separate districts were abolished throughout the state. In Wilmington, rioting in 1967 made it painfully clear to Delawareans just how difficult life was for many blacks and just how strained race-relations were.*

In the 1980s, Delaware achieved an economic boom thanks in part to the Financial Development Center Act which encouraged out-of-state banks to set up shop in Delaware. Increased revenues from banks, businesses incorporated in Delaware, and a relatively high income tax has enabled Delaware to forego the dreaded sales tax. Thanks to no sales tax, visitors are just as liable to think of Delaware as a shopping haven than as the home of the du Ponts. In recent years, development has been the watchword in Delaware. A Sunday drive through Delaware will reveal that pockets of development are occurring from Middletown to the beach--the open spaces and rural texture of downstate Delaware have now made Kent and Sussex the place to live.

*We will begin this journey in 1900 when the first incorporation law
went into effect.*

1. Delaware's national reputation as the place to incorporate is
    not a recent phenomenon. Delaware has been enticing out-of-
    state businesses since 1900, when the General Incorporation
    Law of 1899 went into effect. Out-of-state corporations like
    the fact that the state has a court that is experienced in
    corporate litigation. What is the name of the court?
    a. Chancery   c. Court of Common Pleas
    b. Supreme Court   d. Magistrate

2. Also in 1900, the nationally known illustrator and writer of
    The Merry Adventures of Robin Hood opened an art studio in
    Wilmington. Who was he?
    a. Maxfield Parrish
    b. Norman Rockwell
    c. Howard Pyle
    d. William Morris

3. In 1901, Tom Postles was the first African American elected
    to an office in Delaware. To what office in Wilmington was
    he elected?
    a. mayor
    b. county executive
    c. Wilmington City Council member
    d. county council member

4. It took until 1901 but the General Assembly finally ratified the
    Thirteenth, Fourteenth, and Fifteenth Amendments to the U.S.
    Constitution. Which one of the following is not one of these
    amendments?
    a. right for black suffrage
    b. income tax
    c. forbids slavery
    d. due process clause

5. To benefit farmers, the Baltimore Trust was established in Selbyville in 1903, by a local agricultural entrepreneur who was to become a governor of Delaware. Who was he?
    a. Gove Saulsbury
    b. C. Douglas Buck
    c. William Burton
    d. John G. Townsend

6. The state's first vehicle registration law was a cream puff: take no test, pay two dollars, and provide your own license plate. The maximum speed must have been a thrill for 1905, however. What was it?
    a. 10 mph
    b. 20 mph
    c. 30 mph
    d. 40 mph

7. Delaware took the sabbath day quite seriously in the early twentieth century. In fact, an Arden resident and internationally-known author of *The Jungle*, published 1906, was arrested with friends for playing sports on Sunday. Who was this writer?
    a. Upton Sinclair
    b. F. Scott Fitzgerald
    c. John Steinbeck
    d. Sherwood Anderson

8. In 1912, the present state flag was adopted by the General Assembly. The date that Delaware ratified the Constitution is on the flag. What date is it?
    a. July 4, 1776
    b. December 7, 1787
    c. June 6, 1944
    d. April 12, 1861

9. In 1912, the DuPont Company was broken up in an anti-trust suit which claimed that the company held monopolistic power over the gunpowder industry. Name one of the companies that was formed as a result of this suit.
   a. Chrysler
   b. Baltimore Trust
   c. Hercules Powder
   d. Gore

10. A few years later the DuPont Company made what was to be a profitable investment in a car company. What is the name of this company?
    a. Plymouth
    b. General Motors
    c. Chrysler
    d. Ford

11. In 1914, a new college that was to eventually merge with Delaware College opened in Newark. What was the name of this new college?
    a. Wesley
    b. Newark Academy
    c. Women's College
    d. Delaware State

12. Name the thriving--and still expanding--hospital that opened in Lewes in 1915.
    a. Memorial
    b. St. Francis
    c. Beebe
    d. Kent General

13. In 1915, the Wilmington City Council followed the advice of the NAACP and banned a movie that is a biased account of blacks during the Reconstruction Era. What is the name of this movie?
    a. *Gone With the Wind*
    b. *Birth of a Nation*
    c. *Porgy and Bess*
    d. *Shaft*

14. Led by activist and Howard High School teacher Alice Dunbar Nelson, a chapter of the NAACP was chartered in Wilmington in 1915. Name the renowned scholar and editor of the organization's magazine, *The Crisis*, who helped spearhead the formation of the NAACP in 1909 - 1910.
    a. Ralph Abernathy
    b. Paul Robeson
    c. Booker T. Washington
    d. W. E. B. DuBois

15. In 1916, Josiah O. Wolcott was the first U.S. Senator from Delaware elected by popular vote--thanks to the Seventeenth Amendment. How were senators elected prior to Wolcott?
    a. special convention
    b. electoral college
    c. General Assembly
    d. delegates from the hundreds

16. T. Coleman du Pont started building what is now Route 13 at the southern end of Delaware. By 1917 the first section from the Maryland line to what southern Delaware town was completed?
    a. Laurel
    b. Frankford
    c. Delmar
    d. Selbyville

17. The Delaware National Guard was called to duty in 1918 to fight in Europe during WWI. To what European country were they first sent?
    a. England
    b. Germany
    c. France
    d. Spain

18. In 1918, Delaware became the ninth state to ratify the Eighteenth Amendment. What is the Eighteenth Amendment?
    a. a national income tax
    b. repealed prohibition
    c. the number of terms for the president
    d. women's right to vote

19. In 1926, erosion finally toppled Delaware's first lighthouse. On what beach was this eighteenth-century lighthouse located?
    a. Lewes
    b. Rehoboth
    c. Dewey
    d. Delaware Seashore

20. During the Depression, in Delaware, as in other states, federal agencies were set up to provide work for the unemployed. The WPA was one such program. What does WPA stand for?
    a. Western Political Agency
    b. Works Progress Administration
    c. Wildlife Protection Agency
    d. Wilderness Protection Act

21. Cecile Steele probably had no idea how profitable a business she was starting when she received these farm animals through the mail in 1938. What were they?
    a. broilers
    b. cows
    c. sheep
    d. horses

22. In 1924, Florence M. Hanby achieved a first for Delaware women by being elected to the General Assembly. To what House was she elected?
    a. Senate
    b. House of Representatives

23. In 1927, the federal government deepened and widened the Chesapeake and Delaware Canal. This work removed the need for what in the canal?
    a. tug boats
    b. drawbridges
    c. locks
    d. horse-drawn barges

24. Social welfare interested this du Pont. In 1929, he used his own money to provide pensions for a number of needy senior citizens. Who was he?
    a. Alexis I.
    b. Lammot
    c. T. Coleman
    d. Alfred I.

25. Louis L. Redding went on to a distinguished career after being the first African American to be admitted to the Delaware Bar in 1929. From what prestigious law school did Redding graduate?
    a. Harvard   c. New York
    b. Yale   d. Georgetown

26. When it was completed in 1935 it was the largest school in the state. Name this school named after another du Pont.
    a. A. Felix du Pont
    b. Alfred Victor du Pont
    c. Pierre S. du Pont
    d. T. Coleman du Pont

27. In 1933, the State Welfare Home opened in Smyrna. What does this building house today?
    a. Beebe Hospital
    b. Delaware Home and Hospital for the Chronically Ill
    c. Kent General Hospital
    d. Blue Cross Blue Shield of Delaware

28. Legislative Hall was completed in Dover in 1933. What term best describes the architectural style of Legislative Hall?
    a. Georgian
    b. Gothic
    c. Victorian
    d. Italian Villa

29. Do you know that Delaware owns a piece of New Jersey? The U.S. Supreme Court ruled in 1935 that Penn's twelve mile radius extended to the low-water mark on New Jersey's coast. Thus, Delaware was awarded what national migratory bird refuge?
    a. Killcohook
    b. Bombay
    c. DeSoto
    d. Mille Lacs

30. A rather large crowd assembled to hear this president speak from the rear platform of a train in Wilmington in 1936. Who was he?
    a. Herbert Hoover
    b. Franklin D. Roosevelt
    c. Calvin Coolidge
    d. Harry S. Truman

31. In 1938, Delaware celebrated the three-hundredth anniversary of the landing of the Swedes with a celebration that included the Crown Prince and Princess of Sweden and President Franklin D. Roosevelt. What term describes a three-hundred year celebration?
    a. bicentennial
    b. tricentennial
    c. quadricentennial
    d. centennial

32. In 1939, the DuPont Company open a plant in Seaford to manufacture what product?
    a. nylon
    b. rayon
    c. cellophane
    d. spandex fiber

33. Historian Harold H. Hancock points out that when this Dover plant was established in 1939, it was the first in the area to have nothing to do with agriculture. Name it.
    a. Sears
    b. W. L. Gore
    c. ICI Americas
    d. International Latex

34. The Alfred I. du Pont Institute for Crippled Children (now the Alfred I. du Pont Institute) opened in 1940 on the grounds of Nemours thanks to the efforts of this du Pont widow who is noted for her philantropy as well as her interest in education, landscaping, and architectural restoration. What is her first name?
    a. Eleutnera
    b. Jessie Ball
    c. Bessie
    d. Margaret

35. In recognition of their valor during World War II what medal did William Lloyd Nelson and James P. Conner receive?
    a. Medal of Freedom
    b. Purple Heart
    c. Silver Cross
    d. Medal of Honor

36. When this bridge was built in 1942 over the Chesapeake and Delaware Canal, it replaced a drawbridge. Name the bridge that many feel has seen better days.
    a. Summit Bridge
    b. St. Georges Bridge
    c. Chesapeake City Bridge
    d. Delaware City Bridge

37. In 1943, Howard High School, the Wilmington school for
     blacks, scheduled its first game with a local white school.
     Howard had previously played out-of-state schools. What
     Quaker established school did they play?
     a. Sanford
     b. Wilmington Friends
     c. Ursuline
     d. Archmere

38. Which car company produced the first car made in Delaware,
     in 1947?
     a. General Motors
     b. Chrysler

39. In 1948, a parochial high school was the first all-white school
     to admit black students. Which one was it?
     a. Salesianum
     b. St. Elizabeth's
     c. Padua
     d. St. Mark's

40. In 1948, William J. Winchester was the first African American
     elected to the General Assembly. What party did he represent?
     a. Republican
     b. Democrat

41. In 1951, two business schools merged into one. What is the
     name of this school?
     a. Goldey-Beacom
     b. Wharton
     c. Wesley
     d. Wilmington

42. The whipping post was last used as a form of punishment in
     1952. During what decade was it outlawed as a punishment?
     a. 1950s   c. 1970s
     b. 1960s   d. 1980s

43. In 1952, Chancellor Collins J. Seitz set a legal precedent in Delaware by ruling against segregation in Delaware schools. In a couple of years, this case was to become part of a nationally famous case that was argued before the United States Supreme Court. What is the name of the case argued before the Supreme Court?
    a. *Gitlow v. New York*
    b. *Miranda v. Arizona*
    c. *Gideon v. Wainwright*
    d. *Brown v. the Board of Education of Topeka, Kansas*

44. In 1957, Delaware Bay watermen were disheartened to learn that a microscopic parasite commonly referred to as MSX (multinucleated sphere X) was killing what type of seafood?
    a. clams
    b. crabs
    c. oysters
    d. lobsters

45. It's ironic that an elected official would be denied service in a Wilmington restaurant, but segregation was still prevalent in the late-1950s and the Wilmington City Councilman was African American. Who was he?
    a. William "Dutch" Burton
    b. William "Judy" Johnson
    c. Carter G. Woodson
    d. Paul Robeson

46. In 1963, African Americans were first admitted to what law enforcement agency?
    a. State Police
    b. Wilmington City Police
    c. FBI
    d. Dover Police

47. The same year that John F. Kennedy addressed a crowd at the opening of I-95 outside of Newark, many Delawareans saw a plane fall from the sky killing all eighty passengers. Near what Maryland city did this occur?
    a. Easton   c. Aberdeen
    b. Elkton   d. Chestertown

48. As was the case in many states, legislative representation was not fairly distributed throughout the election districts. Court challenges, the Reapportionment Law of 1964, and state censuses eventually led to more equitable representation. What county most benefitted from reapportionment?
    a. New Castle County
    b. Kent County
    c. Sussex County

49. As they did in many cities, race-related riots broke out in Wilmington in April of 1968 primarily due to the assassination of Martin Luther King, Jr. The National Guard was ordered to patrol Wilmington by Governor Terry and kept there until January of 1969 when the new governor removed the guard. Who was this newly inaugurated governor?
    a. Elbert Carvel
    b. J. Caleb Boggs
    c. Russell Peterson
    d. Sherman W. Tribbitt

50. Prior to 1971 the governor shared administrative duties with more than 140 state agencies, a system that critics charged was becoming increasingly less efficient. What was adopted by the General Assembly in 1971 that dramatically changed the executive branch of government and placed more power in the governor's hands?
    a. lieutenant governor
    b. executive cabinet system
    c. veto power
    d. special sessions

51. In 1973, the city of Wilmington decided to give away for free, old, abandoned houses to people willing to invest time and money in their restoration. What was the name of this successful effort to improve urban communities?
    a. Housing and Urban Development
    b. Habitat for Humanity
    c. Urban Homesteading Project
    d. Save Our Cities

52. In 1974, an elementary class from Milford was responsible for selecting an insect that was eventually adopted by the General Assembly as the state bug. What is the Delaware state bug?
    a. mosquito
    b. wasp
    c. lady bug
    d. beetle

53. In 1976, the state faced a serious financial crisis. A bank in which the state owned a majority interest almost collapsed. What was the name of this bank?
    a. Delaware Trust
    b. Farmers Bank
    c. Bank of Delaware
    d. Delaware Savings

54. In 1977, Thomas R. Carper took office as Delaware's United States Representative, a position he held until 1993 when he was inaugurated as governor. Who was the representative just prior to Carper?
    a. Harris B. McDowell, Jr.
    b. William V. Roth
    c. Pierre S. du Pont IV
    d. Thomas B. Evans, Jr.

55. Ordered by a federal court district judge to achieve racial integration in public schools, New Castle County began busing in 1978. Name the federal judge.
    a. Joseph J. Longobardi
    b. Jane R. Roth
    c. Collins J. Seitz
    d. Murray Schwartz

56. In 1980, the legislature authorized an unprecedented five million dollar loan to a private industry. To whom was the loan authorized?
    a. Rollins
    b. Gore
    c. DuPont
    d. Chrysler

57. Banking is now a major industry in Delaware due largely to the Financial Center Development Act passed by the General Assembly in 1981. The Act offered tax and other incentives to out-of-state banks. Under whose governorship and support was this act passed?
    a. Sherman W. Tribbitt
    b. Pierre S. du Pont IV
    c. Michael N. Castle
    d. Charles L. Terry

58. In 1984, two Wilmington ice skaters won the silver medal in the Olympics at Sarajevo. Who are they?
    a. Elena Valova and Oleg Vassiliev
    b. Kitty and Peter Carruthers
    c. Elisabeth Schwartz and Kurt Oppelt
    d. Andree Joly and Pierre Brunet

59. What Delaware democrat tested the waters for presidency in the 1980s?
    a. J. Allen Frear, Jr.
    b. Pierre S. du Pont IV
    c. Joseph R. Biden
    d. William V. Roth

60. By 1989, half of the companies on this prestigious list were incorporated in Delaware. What is the name of this list?
    a. American Exchange
    b. Dow Jones
    c. New York Exchange
    d. Fortune Five Hundred

61. The 1991 Tour DuPont featured this famous American bicyclist who won the Tour de France three times. Who is he?
    a. Greg LeMond
    b. Andy Hampster
    c. James Moore
    d. Miguel Indurain

62. The 1991 - 92 basketball season proved to be a successful one for the Delaware Blue Hens. They won twenty straight games and won a playoff berth in what well-known tournament?
    a. NHL
    b. NFL
    c. NBA
    d. NCAA

63. In 1992, the University of Delaware completed a sports convocation center. Who is the center named after?
    a. Herbert L. Rice
    b. Tubby Raymond
    c. Bob Carpenter
    d. William D. Murray

64. On January 4, 1992 one of the worst storms in thirty years damaged Delaware resort areas. The name for the type of storm also describes the direction from which it originates. What type of storm was it?
    a. northwester
    b. southwester
    c. northeaster
    d. eastwester

65. In February of 1992, what parochial high school team proved to be a wrestling dynasty when they won the state wrestling tournament for the fifth time in seven years?
    a. St. Mark's
    b. Padua
    c. St. Elizabeth's
    d. Salesianum

66. In 1993, Tom Carper and Mike Castle switched places when Carper became the governor and Castle became Delaware's representative. What office did Castle hold prior to being the governor?
    a. mayor
    b. attorney general
    c. state senator
    d. lieutenant governor

67. Thanks to Tom Carper, visitors to Delaware are greeted with a welcoming sign that reflects the state's status as a shopping mecca. What does the sign say?
    a. First State Shopping
    b. Land of Tax Free Shopping
    c. Home of Tax Free Shopping
    d. Shop Till You Drop

68. Citing family values as a concern, Governor Carper vetoed a bill allowing what type of store to stay open on Sundays?
    a. adult bookstores
    b. liquor stores
    c. pool halls
    d. bars

The Twentieth Century Answers

1.   a.   Chancery

2.   c.   Howard Pyle

3.   c.   Wilmington City Council member

4.   b.   income tax

5.   d.   John G. Townsend

6.   b.   20 mph

7.   a.   Upton Sinclair

8.   b.   December 7, 1787

9.   c.   Hercules Powder

10.   b.   General Motors

11.   c.   Women's College

12.   c.   Beebe

13.   b.   *Birth of a Nation*

14.   d.   W. E. B. DuBois

15.   c.   General Assembly

16.   c.   Delmar

17.   c.   France

18.   d.   women's right to vote

19. a. Lewes

20. b. Works Progress Administration

21. a. broilers

22. b. House of Representatives

23. c. locks

24. d. Alfred I.

25. a. Harvard

26. c. Pierre S. du Pont

27. b. Delaware Home and Hospital for the Chronically Ill

28. a. Georgian

29. a. Killcohook

30. b. Franklin D. Roosevelt

31. b. tercentenary

32. a. nylon

33. d. International Latex

34. b. Jessie Ball

35. d. Medal of Honor

36. b. St. Georges Bridge

37. b. Wilmington Friends

38. a. General Motors

39. a. Salesianum

40. a. Republican

41. a. Goldey-Beacom

42. c. 1970s

43. d. *Brown v. the Board of Education of Topeka, Kansas*

44. c. oysters

45. a. William "Dutch" Burton

46. a. State Police

47. b. Elkton

48. a. New Castle County

49. c. Russell Peterson

50. b. executive cabinet system

51. c. Urban Homesteading Project

52. c. lady bug

53. b. Farmers Bank

54. c. Pierre S. du Pont IV

55. d. Murray Schwartz

56. d. Chrysler

57. b. Pierre S. du Pont IV

58. b. Kitty and Peter Carruthers

59. c. Joseph R. Biden

60. d. Fortune Five Hundred

61. a. Greg LeMond

62. d. NCAA

63. c. Bob Carpenter .

64. c. northeaster

65. a. St. Mark's

66. d. lieutenant governor

67. c. Home of Tax Free Shopping

68. b. liquor stores

Delaware Government

Delaware Government

The imposing Swede, Johan Printz--one of Delaware's earliest governors--didn't need much of a support staff. During his rule from 1641 - 47, he not only made the laws, he also enforced them and meted out justice as he saw fit--often serving as judge, prosecutor, and jury at the same time. This type of one man government has, of course, given way to a more complex system of governing which separates the legislative, executive, and judicial functions of government into three distinct bodies--as outlined in the United States Constitution.

As all state governments do, Delaware government follows the federal model. Its fundamental laws and system of government are outlined in its fourth and present constitution as written in 1897 and as amended many times since then. Delaware's chief executive, the governor, works with twelve cabinet-level departments to provide services for the state's citizens and to enforce the state's laws. Laws are made by Delaware's legislature, the General Assembly, and the judiciary is provided for both in the constitution and by statute with courts ranging from local alderman's courts to the state's highest--the Supreme Court.

Delaware also has dozens of municipal governments which are granted authority by the General Assembly and which provide city services and pass local ordinances. Some of the bigger cities such as Newark and Dover employ full-time city managers to help elected officials--who usually have other jobs--run local governments. Each of Delaware's counties has a system of county government. Although the county governments differ somewhat in structure, they all pass county laws, set property tax rates, provide social services and law enforcement, and run libraries.

Let's begin with the branch that has changed considerably in the last 350 years--the executive.

The Executive Branch

1. Delaware's second constitution (written in 1792) first used the word *governor* to refer to our chief executive. What term did our 1776 constitution use?
   a. chairman
   b. president
   c. chief executive
   d. patroon

2. Under Delaware's first constitution, the governor was not elected by the people, although he was voted in by an elective body. Who elected the governor to office?
   a. State School Board
   b. county councils
   c. General Assembly
   d. Senate

3. According to our present constitution, to qualify to be governor you have to be a citizen and resident of the United States for twelve years and a resident of the state for six years unless absent on public business. What is the minimum age requirement?
   a. thirty
   b. forty
   c. twenty-five
   d. thirty-five

4. What article of the constitution outlines the governor's powers?
   a. I
   b. III
   c. V
   d. VII

5.　If the governor is disabled or dies while in office the lieutenant governor is designated to take his or her place. Who is the third in line of succession according to our constitution?
　　a.　treasurer
　　b.　secretary of state
　　c.　president pro tempore
　　d.　chief justice

6.　One of the lieutenant governor's duties is to preside over one of the houses in the General Assembly. Which one is it?
　　a.　Senate
　　b.　House of Representatives

7.　The governor and the lieutenant governor serve ex-officio on a number of boards and commissions. What does ex-officio mean?
　　a.　by virtue of office
　　b.　out of necessity
　　c.　former official
　　d.　serve with honor

8.　The governor is not the only person elected to the executive branch statewide. Of the five other elective positions, four include the lieutenant governor, the auditor, the treasurer, and the insurance commissioner. What is the last one?
　　a.　chief justice
　　b.　attorney general
　　c.　secretary of state
　　d.　public defender

9.　What is the auditor's chief responsibility?
　　a.　investigates ethics violations
　　b.　issues checks
　　c.　checks financial records
　　d.　prepares the budget

10. The governor addresses the General Assembly at the start of each annual session of the legislature. What is the governor's message called?
    a. annual address
    b. state of the state
    c. governor's address
    d. inaugural speech

11. One of the governor's responsibilities is to estimate state expenses for each fiscal year and recommend to the legislature the amount that should be appropriated. What are the dates for the fiscal year?
    a. July 1 to June 30
    b. January 1 to December 31
    c. April 1 to March 31
    d. September 1 to August 31

12. The governor has the power to fill vacancies in elective offices except for members of the General Assembly and what other office?
    a. auditor
    b. insurance commissioner
    c. treasurer
    d. lieutenant governor

13. In our early state history the governorship was not a particularly powerful office. The General Assembly was much more powerful. Our 1897 constitution gave the governor a power over legislative enactment that he had not previously held. What is that power?
    a. to appoint state officials
    b. veto
    c. ceremonial activities
    d. to recommend commission members

14. The founding fathers of the Delaware State--as it was called in 1776--thought it desirable to limit the powers of the governor simply because colonial governors were too strong. Three of the following answers are suggestive of limited governorial power. Which one shows the strength of the governorship?
    a. term length
    b. other elected executive offices
    c. sharing administrative duties
    d. pardon

15. The governor has the power of line-item veto over one type of bill that earmarks funding for state operations. What type is it?
    a. amendment
    b. general bill
    c. appropriation bill
    d. special bill

16. If the governor decides to veto a bill, it goes back to the house from which it originated. Assuming the bill was passed with a simple majority, what does it take to override a veto?
    a. three-fifths
    b. one-half
    c. seven-eighths
    d. three-fourths

17. A bill could become law without the governor's signature. Unless the legislature has adjourned, the governor only has a certain amount of days (Sundays excepted) to return the bill signed or vetoed--otherwise the bill becomes law. How many days does the governor have?
    a. thirty days
    b. twenty-five days
    c. five days
    d. ten days

18. After the General Assembly has adjourned, the governor has thirty days to act on a bill. If the governor does not sign a bill within that time, it is automatically vetoed and may not be overridden by the General Assembly. This is known as what type of veto?
    a. after session veto
    b. override
    c. line-item
    d. pocket

19. Aside from the regular sessions of the legislature, the governor may call the legislature into session to address pressing business often having to do with the budget. What are these sessions called?
    a. regular sessions
    b. legislative sessions
    c. special sessions
    d. extra sessions

20. Which one of the following is a "legislative" power of the executive branch?
    a. pardon
    b. veto
    c. appointments
    d. commander-in-chief

21. Which of the following is a "judicial" power of the executive branch?
    a. veto
    b. call special sessions
    c. reprieve
    d. make appointments

22. The governor is commander-in-chief of the National Guard. The governor's military power can be superseded, however. Under what circumstances might this occur?
    a. when a senator requests it
    b. when there is a riot
    c. when the governor is out of the state
    d. when the federal government calls the guard into service

23. The governor may, for example, detail the National Guard for duty, establish a commission, or create a task force to study a problem. The governor does this by an official act. What is this act called?
    a. executive order
    b. governor's command
    c. executive privilege
    d. executive directive

24. It would take a two-thirds vote of the House to impeach the governor. What percentage of the vote by the Senate is required for conviction?
    a. three-fourths
    b. one half
    c. two-thirds
    d. one hundred percent

25. In Delaware's history, how many governors have been impeached?
    a. 0   c. 2
    b. 1   d. 5

26. The governor has the power to deliver a person charged with a crime in another state to that state, although the accused has a right to a hearing during which a judge may stay the governor's power. What is the governor's power called?
    a. jurisdiction
    b. extradition
    c. intervention
    d. habeas corpus

27. Of the following, which has to do with the governor's ability to give a lighter sentence?
    a. reprieve
    b. pardon
    c. commutation
    d. forgiveness

28. Along with his executive and administrative duties, the governor is the state's chief host. Official receptions aren't always held at the governor's mansion since it's too small to accommodate large groups. What is the name of the governor's mansion?
    a. David Hall House
    b. The Hermitage
    c. Buena Vista
    d. Woodburn

29. At one time the executive branch of government consisted of dozens of boards and commissions often headed by volunteers, thus making the governor's job more difficult. In 1971, Delaware changed to a cabinet form of government. There are ten cabinet departments. What is the official title of the head of each cabinet department?
    a. superintendent   c. chief
    b. secretary   d. commissioner

30. Cabinet departments are divided into divisions. For example, the Division of Highways is part of the Department of Transportation. Let's see if you can match a few divisions with their departments. Forestry is a division of what department?
    a. Natural Resources and Environmental Control
    b. Department of Agriculture

31. The Division of Alcoholism, Drug Abuse, and Mental Health is part of what department?
    a. Department of Health and Social Services
    b. Department of Public Safety

32. Who heads the Department of State?
    a. auditor
    b. insurance commissioner
    c. lieutenant governor
    d. secretary of state

145

33. What department does the attorney general head?
    a. Department of Justice
    b. Department of Corrections

34. The governor can appoint (with the consent of the Senate) or fire cabinet secretaries or division chiefs. But workers below that level are less subject to the vissicitudes of politics. What protects most state workers?
    a. state merit system
    b. pension
    c. credit union
    d. benefits

35. Who is responsible for "affixing the Great Seal of the State of Delaware" to official documents?
    a. secretary of state
    b. treasurer
    c. auditor
    d. attorney general

36. The Department of Public Instruction is not officially part of the governor's cabinet. The state school superintendent is DPI's chief administrative officer. Who is the governing body of DPI?
    a. Post Secondary Education Committee
    b. the governor
    c. State School Board
    d. General Assembly

37. Who fulfills the executive function in New Castle County government?
    a. commissioner
    b. mayor
    c. county executive
    d. chief executive

38. Arden (along with Ardencroft and Ardentown) has a different governmental style than all other incorporated municipalities in Delaware. What type of governing body does Arden have?
    a. mayor and council
    b. trustees and town meeting
    c. president and commissioners
    d. president and council

39. Who is the chief executive of Dover?
    a. president
    b. comptroller
    c. town manager
    d. mayor

40. Lewes has a mayor and a council. But it also has what other appointed official who shares administrative duties with the mayor?
    a. police chief
    b. treasurer
    c. town manager
    d. secretary

The Executive Branch Answers

1. b. president

2. c. General Assembly

3. a. thirty

4. b. III

5. b. secretary of state

6. a. Senate

7. a. by virtue of office

8. b. attorney general

9. c. checks financial records

10. b. state of the state

11. a. July 1 to June 30

12. d. lieutenant governor

13. b. veto

14. d. pardon

15. c. appropriation bill

16. a. three-fifths

17. d. ten days

18. d. pocket

19. c. special sessions

20. b. veto

21. c. reprieve

22. d. when the federal government calls the guard into service

23. a. executive order

24. c. two-thirds

25. a. 0

26. b. extradition

27. c. commutation

28. d. Woodburn

29. b. secretary

30. b. Department of Agriculture

31. a. Department of Health and Social Services

32. d. secretary of state

33. a. Department of Justice

34. a. state merit system

35. a. secretary of state

36. c. State School Board

37. c. county executive

38. b. trustees and town meeting

39. d. mayor

40. c. town manager

The Legislative Branch

1. Delaware, along with all the other states except for Nebraska, has a two-house legislative system. What term describes a two-house system?
    a. bicameral
    b. dual house
    c. bipartisan
    d. two chambers

2. Delaware's legislature, called the General Assembly, meets at the state's capital in Dover. Name the building where the General Assembly meets.
    a. City Hall
    b. Kent County Courthouse
    c. Legislative Hall
    d. State House

3. The legislature is divided into two houses--upper and lower. Which one is the upper house?
    a. Senate
    b. House of Representatives

4. Article II of the state's constitution outlines the powers and makeup of the legislature. According to the constitution the minimum age requirement to be a state representative is 24. What is the minimum age requirement to be a state senator?
    a. 24
    b. 27
    c. 30
    d. 35

5. What is the term of office for a state representative?
    a. one year   c. four years
    b. two years   d. six years

6. What is the term of office for a state senator?
   a. one year
   b. four years
   c. five years
   d. six years

7. The General Assembly has the power to create legislative districts. How often are legislative districts reapportioned if population changes require new legislative boundary lines?
   a. every five years
   b. every ten years
   c. every twenty-five years
   d. every fifty years

8. Because of a 1964 United States Supreme Court decision, legislative districts in every state must be apportioned on the basis of population. Also, by law in Delaware, districts must not be created to favor any particular party, once a common practice in many states. What term describes the process of creating districts to favor a particular party?
   a. voter manipulation
   b. gerrymandering
   c. bipartisan
   d. election fraud

9. How are legislative nominees picked in Delaware?
   a. popular vote   b. by convention

10. According to the constitution, the regular session of the legislature must occur once a year for about six months. The regular session convenes on the second Tuesday of each January. When must the regular session end?
    a. at midnight on April 15
    b. at midnight on May 15
    c. at midnight on June 30
    d. at midnight on September 30

11. Each house has a presiding officer whose chief responsibility is to conduct the business of the house floor, refer bills to committee, and make committee assignments. Who is the presiding officer of the House of Representatives?
     a. majority whip
     b. speaker of the house
     c. president pro tempore
     d. lieutenant governor

12. When the presiding officer of the senate is absent, who is responsible for conducting business?
     a. president pro tempore
     b. minority whip
     c. speaker of the house
     d. lieutenant governor

13. One of the majority party's leaders has the job of making sure party members vote and attend caucuses. What is the title of this aptly named party leader?
     a. majority leader
     b. party boss
     c. committee chairperson
     d. whip

14. A simple majority of members for each house must be present for the house to conduct business. What is the term to describe the necessary number of members?
     a. caucus
     b. majority
     c. quorum
     d. sufficient amount

15. Legislators may be required to not vote on a bill. Under what circumstances might this occur? If the legislator:
     a. has not attended all sessions during which the bill was discussed.
     b. has a personal interest in the bill.
     c. is not on the committee from which it originated.
     d. has no expertise on the bill's subject matter.

16. Legislators may take different types of votes during a session. Which type describes saying aye or no aloud?
    a. teller vote
    b. record vote
    c. viva vote
    d. standing vote

17. Bills may originate from many different sources, such as the government (the governor's office, for example) or the private sector (lobbyists or citizens with special interests). No bill, however, will be considered by the General Assembly unless a representative introduces it. The representative who introduces the bill is referred to as the bill's what?
    a. sponsor
    b. advisor
    c. director
    d. supporter

18. Before bills are considered by the General Assembly as a whole, they are sent to a committee for review and debate. Not all bills that committees receive reach the floor of a house. In fact, most never do. How does a bill get "reported out" of a committee to reach the floor of a house?
    a. the committee chairperson decides
    b. majority vote in the committee
    c. the governor calls for it
    d. unanimous vote in the committee

19. After bills reach a committee, who decides when they will be discussed?
    a. a member of the majority party
    b. the chairman
    c. a member of the minority party
    d. party whip

20. A bill that is not reported out may reach the full chamber if the chamber by a majority vote requests it. What is this process known as?
    a. petitioning out
    b. override
    c. veto
    d. chamber bypass

21. Special committees may be formed to study a particular bill under consideration. However, some committees meet permanently--education, ethics, and revenue and taxation are examples. What are these committees called?
    a. financial committee
    b. legislative committee
    c. joint committee
    d. standing committee

22. Committees may be made up of members of a single house or members of both houses. What is a committee made up of both houses called?
    a. joint committee
    b. standing committee
    c. bipartisan committee
    d. full house committee

23. One very important committee has the responsibility for studying the governor's proposed budget. What is this committee called?
    a. Judiciary Committee
    b. Joint Sunset Committee
    c. Joint Finance Committee
    d. Bond Bill Committee

24. The General Assembly always allots a portion of the state finances to non-profit organizations. By what means is this done?
    a. bond bill
    b. grants-in-aid bill
    c. special bill
    d. amendment

25. One committee consisting of members of both houses meets to determine if certain state agencies are still necessary. What is this committee called?
    a. House Administration Committee
    b. Human Resources Committee
    c. Sunset Committee
    d. Labor and Pension Committee

26. The General Assembly also has the power to amend the state constitution. To pass an amendment, each house of the General Assembly must pass the amendment with a two-thirds vote for two successive sessions. The amendment process in Delaware differs from every other state. In what way does it differ?
    a. Amendments are passed by popular votes in other states.
    b. Amendments are passed by legislators in one session.

27. Which of the following is an "executive" power of the General Assembly?
    a. vote on bills
    b. committee work
    c. amend state constitution
    d. confirmation of judges

28. Which one of the following is a "judicial" power of the General Assembly?
    a. power to expel a member
    b. override a veto
    c. vote on a simple resolution
    d. ratify amendments to the U.S. Constitution

29. Although it has never been done in Delaware, the legislature has the power to impeach and try the governor. Which house has the power to impeach and which house has the power to try the governor?
    a. The House has the power to impeach; the Senate has the power to try.
    b. The Senate has the power to impeach; the House has the power to try.

30. The governor has the power to appoint judges. Which house has the power to confirm them?
    a. Senate
    b. House of Representatives

31. Statutes--and resolutions passed by the legislature, as well as proclamations by the governor--are published as soon as possible after the regular session adjourns. What cabinet department has the responsibility for compiling this information for publication?
    a. labor
    b. finance
    c. administrative services
    d. state

32. Like most modern legislatures, the General Assembly has a group which assists with bill drafting, research, and other legislative duties that Delaware legislators--many of whom work other jobs--have little time for. What is this group called?
    a. Legislative Council
    b. lobbyists
    c. Ethics Committee
    d. Research Council

33. We'll end with a few questions about local and county governments. Each county in Delaware has a different form of government. In New Castle County, the county executive with his or her staff performs administrative and executive functions for the county. What group of seven performs the legislative function for New Castle County?
    a. commissioners
    b. county representatives
    c. county council
    d. levy court

34. In Kent County the legislative and executive functions are performed by a group of seven elected commissioners who work with county administrators and other staff. What is this type of government known as?
    a. trustees
    b. levy court
    c. county council
    d. leaseholders

35. The governing body of Sussex County consists of five elected representatives who must meet every week and who appoint an administrator to run the county's daily affairs. What is this governing body called?
    a. county council
    b. the commission
    c. legislative assembly
    d. executive branch

36. There are over fifty incorporated municipalities in Delaware functioning under charters granted by the General Assembly. Laws passed by municipal councils are not called statutes since they don't have statewide jurisdiction. What are local laws called?
    a. misdemeanors
    b. ordinances
    c. laws
    d. city rules

The Legislative Branch Answers

1. a. bicameral

2. c. Legislative Hall

3. a. Senate

4. b. 27

5. b. two years

6. b. four years

7. b. every ten years

8. b. gerrymandering

9. b. by convention

10. c. at midnight on June 30

11. b. speaker of the house

12. a. president pro tempore

13. d. whip

14. c. quorum

15. b. has a personal interest in the bill.

16. c. viva vote

17. a. sponsor

18. b. majority vote in the committee

19. b. the chairman

20. a. petitioning out

21. d. standing committee

22. a. joint committee

23. c. Joint Finance Committee

24. b. grants-in-aid bill

25. c. Sunset Committee

26. a. Amendments are passed by popular vote in other states.

27. d. confirmation of judges

28. a. power to expel a member

29. a. The House has the power to impeach; the Senate has the power to try.

30. a. Senate

31. d. secretary of state

32. a. Legislative Council

33. c. county council

34. b. levy court

35. a. county council

36. b. ordinances

The Judicial Branch

1. Let's start with a few basic questions about our legal system. In a criminal case, guilt or innocence is determined in a trial. A trial, however, is not used to determine the outcome of a civil action. Which term denotes a trial for a civil action?
   a. hearing
   b. pleading
   c. suit
   d. small claims

2. In a criminal case one party is the person accused of the crime. Who is the other party in a criminal case?
   a. the state
   b. victim
   c. plaintiff
   d. magistrate

3. Other than in Wilmington, if a suspect is arrested he or she is taken to a specific court for an initial appearance and bail hearing. What court is this?
   a. Superior Court
   b. Family Court
   c. Court of Common Pleas
   d. Justice of the Peace

4. You can't bring someone to trial in a criminal case unless there is enough evidence. A grand jury decides if there is enough evidence to bring a person charged with a crime to trial. How many grand juries are in the State of Delaware?
   a. one
   b. three
   c. five
   d. seven

5. A grand jury has to be rather official scheduling someone for a trial if they decide the evidence warrants it. What must they "pass down" before scheduling the accused?
   a. de novo
   b. complaint
   c. indictment
   d. writ of mandamus

6. The type of jury that is most familiar is the one that sits in judgment in a criminal or civil case. What is this type of jury called?
   a. citizen jury
   b. hung jury
   c. grand jury
   d. petit jury

7. A criminal case may end with finding the defendant guilty--a conviction--or not guilty. A not guilty verdict is referred to as what?
   a. an indictment
   b. an acquittal
   c. benign outcome
   d. no-fault

8. Here's a tough one. What is a voir dire examination?
   a. the process of jury selection
   b. the process of selecting witnesses
   c. the process of swearing in witnesses
   d. plea bargaining

9. A justice of the peace is a lay judge. What type of judge presides over a higher court?
   a. chief justice
   b. magistrate
   c. law
   d. trial

10. Judges base decisions and punishments on statutory law--laws enacted by the General Assembly. However, judges may also be guided by decisions passed down from other judges--judge-made law. What is judge-made law known as?
   a. common law
   b. constitutional law
   c. criminal law
   d. civil law

11. Once a judge makes a decision he or she sets a precedent for similar cases to follow. Judges will generally follow precedents unless they find compelling reasons to reject the precedent and set a new one. That is, judges apply the rule of "let the decision stand." What Latin term describes this rule?
   a. habeas corpus
   b. in camera
   c. mandamus
   d. stare decisis

12. A judge can issue an order prohibiting someone from a specific action--such as harassing someone. What is this order called?
   a. advisory opinion
   b. injunction
   c. declaratory judgement
   d. writ

13. Delaware's Bill of Rights (Article I of the State Constitution) protects the civil rights of its citizens. The Delaware Bill of Rights, however, says nothing about freedom of speech, as does the First Amendment of the United States Constitution. The First Amendment protects our freedom to speak freely from federal government intervention. Which amendment to the United States Constitution protects freedom of speech from action by Delaware government?
   a. Tenth   c. Fifteenth
   b. Fourteenth   d. Twentieth

14. Section 5 of the Delaware Bill of Rights protects citizens from unreasonable search and seizure. What amendment to the United States Constitution provides the same protection?
    a. Second
    b. Fourth
    c. Eighth
    d. Tenth

15. Which came first: the Delaware Bill of Rights or the United States Bill of Rights?
    a. United States
    b. Delaware

16. Some of the courts in Delaware were established in the constitution. Which one of the following was not?
    a. Justice of the Peace
    b. Superior
    c. Family Court
    d. Chancery

17. By what legal means were courts not in the constitution created?
    a. judicial convention
    b. stare decisis
    c. statute
    d. common law

18. Justices of the Supreme Court, Court of Chancery, and Superior Court are appointed by the governor and confirmed by the Senate. How long do their terms run?
    a. five years
    b. twelve years
    c. fifteen years
    d. lifetime

19. Justice of the peace courts in Delaware have a long tradition dating back to colonial times. These courts handle misdemeanor cases, traffic offenses, and minor civil cases. What is the official title of a Justice of the Peace court judge?
    a. magistrate
    b. circuit judge
    c. alderman
    d. chancellor

20. If you wish to contest a speeding ticket given within the city limits of Newark or Rehoboth, which court would you go to?
    a. City Hall
    b. Justice of the Peace
    c. Family Court
    d. Alderman's

21. Courts such as the Justice of the Peace Courts and Court of Common Pleas are courts of limited jurisdiction since they are restricted as to the type of cases they can hear. Which court serves as the intermediate appellate court for courts of limited jurisdiction?
    a. Superior Court
    b. Justice of the Peace
    c. Family Court
    d. Supreme Court

22. What city has a Municipal Court?
    a. Dover
    b. Newark
    c. Wilmington
    d. Georgetown

23. Family Court has jurisdiction over cases involving juveniles and family matters such as divorce and child neglect. How many Family Courts are in Delaware?
    a. one   c. five
    b. three   d. ten

24   Family Court hears cases involving juveniles, unless the
     juvenile is accused of first degree murder, kidnapping, or
     which of the following?
     a.   rape
     b.   armed robbery
     c.   breaking and entering
     d.   insurrection

25. Serious crimes such as murder or armed robbery are called
     felonies. What are minor offenses such as speeding and public
     drunkenness called?
     a.   minor crimes
     b.   offenses
     c.   misdemeanors
     d.   criminal acts

26. Let's say someone is suspected of committing a felony,
     arrested, booked, and given a preliminary hearing. What is
     the next step?
     a.   the suspect goes to trial
     b.   the case goes to a grand jury
     c.   the suspect is indicted
     d.   the Attorney General conducts an investigation

27. Felonies can only be heard in which court?
     a.   Family Court
     b.   Common Pleas Court
     c.   Supreme Court
     d.   Superior Court

28. The Court of Chancery has jurisdiction over equity cases.
     What title is given to a Chancery Court judge?
     a.   magistrate
     b.   chancellor
     c.   chief judge
     d.   arbiter

---

29. What does *equity* mean?
    a. civil dispute
    b. fairness
    c. advice
    d. equal

30. The Supreme Court of Delaware is the state's highest court. What is the chief responsibility of the Supreme Court?
    a. to hear appeals
    b. to hear murder cases
    c. to hear equity cases
    d. to monitor other courts

31. The Supreme Court has the power to issue a writ of mandamus. What is a writ of mandamus?
    a. a court order compelling a government official to perform his/her duty
    b. a court order requesting records
    c. a court order prohibiting a specific action
    d. a court order permitting a search

32. How many judges serve on the Delaware Supreme Court?
    a. two
    b. three
    c. five
    d. seven

33. Supreme Court justices are appointed by the governor and confirmed by the Senate. For what length of time are they appointed?
    a. four years
    b. six years
    c. ten years
    d. twelve years

34. If requested, the Delaware Supreme Court can offer an advisory opinion on legal or constitutional matters. Who is the one person who may request an advisory opinion?
    a. governor
    b. lieutenant governor
    c. attorney general
    d. treasurer

35. Delaware also has one of the ninety-one United States District Courts which were created to hear federal cases. These District Courts are divided into eleven circuits. Delaware is part of what federal judicial circuit?
    a. second
    b. third
    c. fifth
    d. tenth

36. Which one of the following cases is a United States District Court not likely to hear?
    a. counterfeiting
    b. child custody
    c. mail fraud
    d. federal tax fraud

The Judicial Branch Answers

1.   c.   suit

2.   a.   the state

3.   d.   Justice of the Peace

4.   b.   three

5.   c.   indictment

6.   d.   petit jury

7.   b.   an acquittal

8.   a.   the process of jury selection

9.   c.   law

10.   a.   common law

11.   d.   stare decisis

12.   b.   injunction

13.   a.   Fourteenth

14.   b.   Fourth

15.   b.   Delaware

16.   c.   Family Court

17.   c.   statute

18.   b.   twelve years

19.   a.   magistrate

20.   d.   Alderman's

21.   a.   Superior Court

22.   c.   Wilmington

23.   b.   three

24.   a.   rape

25.   c.   misdemeanors

26.   b.   the case goes to a grand jury

27.   d.   Superior Court

28.   b.   chancellor

29.   b.   fairness

30.   a.   to hear appeals

31.   a.   a court order compelling a government official to perform his/her duty

32.   c.   five

33.   d.   twelve years

34.   a.   governor

35.   b.   third

36.   b.   child custody

Delaware People

Delaware People

For Delawareans, the "ride" is Caesar Rodney's--the one he made to Philadelphia on the night of July 1, 1776, to cast Delaware's fate with the patriots. Sick and suffering from face cancer, Rodney's journey from Dover that stormy night was no mean feat, although time and some good poetry have given Revere's ride the upperhand in our national consciousness. To their credit, Delaware's school children seem to have no problem giving both heroes their due.

Rodney's heroic ride overshadows his many accomplishments as a public figure. Dedicating himself to public life in his early twenties, Rodney served Delaware in both Continental Congresses, in its General Assembly, as its governor, and as a state supreme court justice. Fortunately, Delaware has had its share of people--past and present--who have served the state well, much in the tradition of Caesar Rodney. It goes without saying that Delaware is a better state because of the many people who have labored, often anonymously, to make Delaware a better place to live.

Delaware also has had no shortage of creative and athletically gifted people--many of whom have achieved national prominence. From drama to rock and roll, Delaware's creative, enrich the state with their artistic talents. And it's no accident that professional scouts keep an eye on Delaware's colleges, universities, and high schools for prospective stars since many Delaware athletes have played professional sports with great success.

Let's start with a University of Delaware professor who has been in the political spotlight.

Public Servants

1. At the time he was elected lieutenant governor in 1984, he held the highest office of any Asian American in the United States. Who is he?
    a. Rae Dong Chong
    b. I.M. Pei
    c. S.B. Woo
    d. Deigi Ozawa

2. Many people were surprised when thirty-year-old Joseph R. Biden beat a popular incumbent in 1973 to become a United States senator. Whom did Biden beat?
    a. J. Caleb Boggs
    b. J. Allen Frear
    c. C. Douglas Buck
    d. John J. Williams

3. Name the African-American state senator from Wilmington who was Delaware's first black state senator.
    a. James M. Baker
    b. James Sills
    c. Al O. Plant
    d. Herman M. Holloway, Sr.

4. Older Delawareans will remember that prior to William Roth he was the only United States senator from Delaware to serve four terms (1946 - 1970). Who is he?
    a. J. Frank Allee
    b. Thomas F. Bayard
    c. John J. Williams
    d. Eli Saulsbury

5. She was elected Delaware's first female lieutenant governor in 1992. Who is she?
    a. Ruth Ann Minner
    b. Emma Belle Gibson Sykes
    c. Arva Jean Jackson
    d. Evelyn Marlin Lord

6. We are indebted to this colonial Delawarean and Pennsylvanian for serving the state in so many capacities. For this question we will just identify him as the "Penman of the Revolution." Who was he?
    a. Thomas McKean
    b. John Vining
    c. George Read
    d. John Dickinson

7. In the early 1970s, this governor's efforts resulted in the passage of the Coastal Zone Act which prohibited the development of industries, particularly oil, along Delaware's shoreline. Who is he?
    a. Elbert N. Carvel
    b. Russell W. Peterson
    c. Thomas R. Carper
    d. Sherman W. Tribbitt

8. Smyrna residents elected the first black mayor in the state in 1981. Who is he?
    a. Kenneth Gibson
    b. Thomas Bradley
    c. George Wright
    d. David Dinkins

9. In the early 1970s, a research group sent to Delaware by this nationally known consumer advocate published a book criticizing the DuPont Company for its extensive influence in state affairs. Who is this advocate?
   a. Lorraine Fleming
   b. Jacob Kreshtool
   c. Ralph Nader
   d. Herb Denenberg

10. Among her many accomplishments, she was instrumental in starting the Delaware Red Cross and combating tuberculosis. She is most known for designing the country's first Christmas seal to raise money to fight TB. Who was she?
    a. Emily P. Bissell
    b. Jean Kane Foulke du Pont
    c. Shirley Tarrant
    d. Elizabeth Yates

11. Because this lawyer and judge was a tireless advocate for the establishment of free schools in the early 1800s, he earned the title "Father of Public Schools." Who was he?
    a. Willard Hall
    b. Evert Pietersen
    c. H. Fletcher Brown
    d. Collins J. Seitz

12. Arva Jackson was the first black appointed to the board of what institution of higher learning in Delaware in 1969?
    a. Delaware State University
    b. Wesley College
    c. University of Delaware
    d. Wilmington College

13. This untypical first lady commuted to Washington and worked for the Reagan administration while her husband was governor. Who is she?
    a. Elise du Pont
    b. Jeanne Tribbitt
    c. Lillian Peterson
    d. Martha Castle

14. Which du Pont is given credit for founding the modern public school system in Delaware?
    a. Henry Francis du Pont
    b. Samuel F. du Pont
    c. Lammot du Pont
    d. Pierre S. du Pont

15. The nation, let alone Delaware, had never seen a highway quite like it when Route 13 was completed in 1924. The du Pont who conceived the idea, financed it, and built much of it before turning it over to the state said that he was going to build a monument over one hundred miles long and lay it on the ground. Who was he?
    a. Alfred I. du Pont
    b. T. Coleman du Pont
    c. Victor du Pont
    d. Irenée du Pont

16. A number of Delaware abolitionists were instrumental in helping slaves escape from the South to the North through Delaware which was also a slave state. Name the Wilmington Quaker and merchant who worked with former slave Harriet Tubman to help slaves escape from the South.
    a. Warner Mifflin
    b. Thomas Garrett
    c. William Shipley
    d. John Hunn

17. A slave from Dover, this preacher bought his freedom and eventually moved to Philadelphia where he started the African Methodist Episcopal Church in 1816. Name him.
    a. Thomas E. Postles
    b. William J. Winchester
    c. William Furrowh
    d. Richard Allen

18. Name the first African American elected to the state legislature (the House of Representatives in 1948).
    a. John O. Hopkins
    b. Al O. Plant
    c. William Winchester
    d. Samuel Burris

19. This noted African-American educator became the first black principal of Howard High School in 1876. Who was she?
    a. Hilda Marie Lockwood Parker
    b. Alice Dunbar Nelson
    c. Edwina B. Kruse
    d. Pauline A. Young

20. Another black educator, NAACP leader, and nationally known civil rights lecturer, taught English at Howard High School. She was also the widow of a famous African-American poet. Who was she?
    a. Phyllis Wheatley
    b. Maya Angelou
    c. Gwendolyn Brooks
    d. Alice Dunbar Nelson

21. This twentieth-century black lawyer won many civil rights lawsuits in Delaware, including a case that was to become part of *Brown v. the Board of Education of Topeka, Kansas*. He was also the state's first black attorney. Who is he?
    a. Harmon Carey
    b. Louis L. Redding
    c. Jerome H. Holland
    d. James Newton

22. Residents of Wilmington's Little Italy regard Father Francis Tucker highly for his work in the community after World War I. Father Tucker was instrumental in having what church built in Wilmington?
    a. St. Mary's
    b. St. Elizabeth's
    c. St. Peter's
    d. St. Anthony's

23. Among her many accomplishments as an astronomer, she published a reference book of thousands of stars. Name the woman from Dover who was known as the "Census Taker of the Sky."
    a. Annie Jump Cannon
    b. Etta J. Wilson
    c. Jessie Ball du Pont
    d. Elizabeth Caulk

24. This Brandywine Hundred Republican was elected to the General Assembly in 1924 as the first woman to serve in the state legislature. Who was she?
    a. Florence M. Hanby
    b. Vera Gilbride Davis
    c. Louise Thompson Connor
    d. Miriam E. Howard

25. John Haslet, a Dover doctor, was the first leader of the Delaware regiment during what war?
     a. French and Indian War
     b. Revolutionary War
     c. 1812 War
     d. Civil War

26. In 1813 this Delawarean was appointed the first surgeon general of the United States Army. Who was he?
     a. Benjamin F. Shaw
     b. John McKinley
     c. David Hall
     d. James Tilton

27. This inventor from Newport worked with steam engines and machinery to move grain in flour mills. Who was he?
     a. Cyrus McCormick
     b. Robert Fulton
     c. Rudolf Diesel
     d. Oliver Evans

28. Name the Quaker textile manufacturer who backed up his belief in maintaining open spaces for public enjoyment by donating valuable land along the Brandywine River. He is recognized as the "Founder" of the New Castle County park system.
     a. Richard J. Neutra
     b. Benjamin H. Latrobe
     c. Frederick Law Olmstead
     d. William Poole Brancroft

29. Wilmington really took off when a wealthy Quaker merchant moved there in 1735 and founded a market. Who was he?
     a. William Shipley
     b. Nicholas Van Dyke
     c. Richard Nicolls
     d. David Hall

30   DuPont chemist Wallace Hume Carothers is noted for developing what product?
    a.   rayon
    b.   nylon
    c.   synthetic resin
    d.   dynamite

31.   As secretary of the Delaware Department of Natural Resources during the Castle administration, this environmentalist ruffled a few feathers with his aggressive pro-environmental policies. Who is he?
    a.   Edwin "Toby" Clark II
    b.   Jacob Kreshtool
    c.   Henry David Thoreau
    d.   Russell W. Peterson

32.   Wilmington-born Daniel Nathans won science's most prestigious prize in 1978 for his work with gene-mapping. What prize did he win?
    a.   Spingarn
    b.   Pulitzer
    c.   Nobel
    d.   Emmy

33.   John Bassett Moore, born in Smyrna, wrote books on international law and was an international jurist at the Hague. Where is the Hague located?
    a.   Ireland
    b.   Germany
    c.   Netherlands
    d.   Switzerland

34. Although Representative Daniel Weiss' attempt to pass legislation in 1974 to improve the conditions of certain workers failed, his crusading efforts eventually resulted in better treatment for these laborers. Who are they?
    a. roofers
    b. fast food workers
    c. construction workers
    d. migrant laborers

35. After many years of distinctive service as the chief justice of the Delaware Supreme Court, this retired judge died in a tragic car accident in New Mexico in 1993. Name the highly regarded judge.
    a. Henry du Pont Ridgely
    b. Samuel Chew
    c. Andrew D. Christie
    d. Richard S. Rodney

36. In 1980, he was appointed the State Superintendent of Education--the first University of Delaware graduate to achieve the position. Who is he?
    a. James H. Groves
    b. H. V. Holloway
    c. William B. Keene
    d. Pat Forgione

37. In 1985, who became the first woman from Delaware appointed a federal judge?
    a. Norma Handloff
    b. Jane Roth
    c. Louise Thompson Connor
    d. Roslyn Rettew

38.	No smoking please--name the insurance commissioner who
	believed that "smokers should pay more for health insurance."
	a.	Daniel O. Hastings
	b.	David P. Buckson
	c.	John L. Sullivan
	d.	David Levinson

39.	Lydia E. Clark (her Native American name was Nau-gwa-ok-
	wa) died in 1856. She has the distinction of being the last
	descendant of the Delaware Indians to speak a language
	common to the Delaware Indians. What is the language?
	a.	Nanticoke
	b.	Osibwe
	c.	Algonquin
	d.	Seneca

40.	You can't call yourself a University of Delaware graduate
	unless you can name the man who served as its president
	(beginning 1968) during its greatest period of expansion. Who
	is he?
	a.	William Samuel Carlson
	b.	John Alanson Perkins
	c.	Edward Arthur Trabant
	d.	Walter Hullihen

41.	During the nineteenth century, three men from Delaware
	served as United States secretaries of state. Which one of the
	following did not?
	a.	Louis McLane
	b.	John M. Clayton
	c.	Nicholas Van Dyke
	d.	Thomas F. Bayard

Public Servants Answers

1. c. S.B. Woo

2. a. J. Caleb Boggs

3. d. Herman M. Holloway, Sr.

4. c. John J. Williams

5. a. Ruth Ann Minner

6. d. John Dickinson

7. b. Russell W. Peterson

8. c. George Wright

9. c. Ralph Nader

10. a. Emily P. Bissell

11. a. Willard Hall

12. c. University of Delaware

13. a. Elise du Pont

14. d. Pierre S. du Pont

15. b. T. Coleman du Pont

16. b. Thomas Garrett

17. d. Richard Allen

18. c. William Winchester

19. c.   Edwina B. Kruse

20. d.   Alice Dunbar Nelson

21. b.   Louis L. Redding

22. d.   St. Anthony's

23. a.   Annie Jump Cannon

24. a.   Florence M. Hanby

25. b.   Revolutionary War

26. d.   James Tilton

27. d.   Oliver Evans

28. d.   William Poole Brancroft

29. a.   William Shipley

30. b.   nylon

31. a.   Edwin "Toby" Clark II

32. c.   Nobel

33. c.   Netherlands

34. d.   migrant laborers

35. c.   Andrew D. Christie

36. c.   William B. Keene

37. b.   Jane Roth

38. d. David Levinson

39. a. Nanticoke

40. c. Edward Arthur Trabant

41. c. Nicholas Van Dyke

The Creative

1. This African-American jazz trumpeter from Wilmington attained international fame before his untimely death in a car accident in 1956 at the age of 26. Name him.
    a. Bix Beiderbecke
    b. Dizzy Gillespie
    c. Clifford Brown
    d. Miles Davis

2. When local musicians speak of "Boysie" they often do so in admiration for one of the best jazz instructors in the region. Who is Boysie?
    a. Gerald Chavis
    b. Robert Lowery
    c. Hal Schiff
    e. Dennis Sandole

3. Former Wilmington city policeman and jazz vibraphonist Lee Winchester ended a promising jazz career by shooting himself with a gun he thought was unloaded. In 1958, Winchester was invited to play at the country's most prestigious jazz festival. Which one was it?
    a. Philadelphia
    b. Chicago
    c. New York
    d. Newport

4. Another Wilmington-raised musician has achieved legendary status among local jazz fans. Name the Los Angeles based saxophonist who has recorded albums and who played on the *Tonight Show* when Johnny Carson was the host.
    a. Ben Webster
    b. Gerry Mulligan
    c. Julian "Cannonball" Adderley
    d. Ernie Watts

5. George Thorogood is Delaware's most famous rock and roll star. Thorogood's band members are also Delawareans. What is the name of his band?
   a. The Destroyers
   b. The Bombers
   c. The Rocks
   d. The Wizards

6. This rock guitarist from Hockessin received national acclaim in the 1970s for his guitar wizardry. His real name is Tom Miller, but he adopted the last name of a famous French poet. Name the poet.
   a. de Musset
   b. Verlaine
   c. Baudelaire
   d. de la Fontaine

7. Johnny Neal achieved national success as a songwriter and as a member of what highly acclaimed band?
   a. Lynyrd Skynyrd
   b. Allman Brothers
   c. Little Feat
   d. Dixie Hummingbirds

8. Many critics credit this reggae star who lived in Wilmington with almost single-handedly creating a surge of national interest in reggae music. Name him.
   a. Peter Tosh
   b. Greg Isaacs
   c. Bob Marley
   d. Ziggy Marley

9. In the mid-1980s, New Castle metal guitarist Vinnie Moore played some hot licks on commercials for what soft drink company?
   a. Coca Cola   c. 7-Up
   b. Pepsi   d. Dr. Pepper

10. Let's turn our attention to the written word. From 1927 - 1929, this famous writer of *The Great Gatsby* lived just north of Wilmington. Who was he?
    a. John Steinbeck
    b. Sherwood Anderson
    c. F. Scott Fitzgerald
    d. Richard Wright

11. Which black writer and educator chronicled growing up on the east side of Wilmington in his 1934 publication, *No Day of Triumph*?
    a. Ralph Ellison
    b. James Baldwin
    c. Richard Wright
    d. J. Saunders Redding

12. A popular *News Journal* columnist went to Vietnam in the 1960s to cover the war. Who was he?
    a. Bill Frank
    b. W. Emerson Wilson
    c. Norman A. Lockman
    d. John H. Taylor

13. Another present *News Journal* political columnist is known to have ruffled a few feathers with his comments on the local political scene. Who is he?
    a. Don Flood
    b. Ralph Moyed
    c. Otto Dekom
    d. Jim Miller

14. This *Delaware State News* humor columnist entertained his readers for many years. Who was he?
    a. Robert Montgomery Bird
    b. Bob Woodward
    c. Jim Miller
    d. Andy Rooney

15. Name the Wilmington-born nineteenth-century African-American woman who is credited with being the first black woman editor in North America.
    a. Shirley Chisholm
    b. Alexa Canady
    c. Mary Ann Shadd Carey
    d. Barbara Harris

16. She began her "Of This and That" column for the *Wilmington Morning News* (now the *News Journal*) in 1953. Her popular column often expressed her concern for the elderly and handicapped. Name the writer.
    a. Sylvia Path
    b. Betty Burroughs
    c. Joyce Carol Oates
    d. Anna T. Lincoln

17. Let's go back a century to a journalist from Georgetown whose most successful novel--*The Entailed Hat* (1884)--tells the story of Delaware's infamous slavenapper, Patty Cannon. Who wrote the book?
    a. James Adams
    b. Francis Vincent
    c. Christopher L. Ward
    d. George Alfred Townsend

18. A few Delawareans have acted in movies and television. Two of the most noted are Teri Polo from Dover and Judge Reinhold from Wilmington. A third is a Wilmington-born actress who starred in the popular TV series, *One Day at a Time*. Who is she?
    a. Teri Polo
    b. Valerie Bertinelli
    c. Kathleen Widdoes
    d. Marie Swajewski

19. This University of Delaware graduate has become a familiar face on local TV as the Channel 12 television anchor. Who is she?
    a. Alfie Moss
    b. Nancy Karibjanian
    c. Phyllis Wood Anderson
    d. Sue Serio

20. Name the Claymont High and University of Delaware graduate who broadcasts on Channel 29.
    a. Lisa Thomas Laury
    b. Diane Allen
    c. Jill Chernekoff
    d. Nora Muchanic

21. This successful director of the documentary *The Civil War* lived in Delaware as a child in the 1950s when his father was a University of Delaware professor. Name him.
    a. Robert Flaherty
    b. Pare Lorentz
    c. David Attenborough
    d. Ken Burns

22. Name the straight-talking and controversial radio and television personality who hosted a show on WILM in the 1950s before going on to host his own television show.
    a. Joe Pyne
    b. H. V. Kaltenborn
    c. Father Charles E. Coughlin
    d. Fred Allen

23. Rehoboth resident Doug James wrote "How Am I Supposed to Live Without You" for what recording artist?
    a. Anita Baker
    b. Laura Branigan
    c. Whitney Houston
    d. Kate Bush

24. In 1983, this nationally known sculptor and Delaware resident completed his version of Madonna which was exhibited in Rodney Square before being moved to California. Who is he?
    a. Robert Shaw
    b. Frank Stephens
    c. Charles Parks
    d. Felix O. C. Darley

25. This African-American artist from Wilmington got his start with the Works Progress Administration in the 1930s and has exhibited in major galleries throughout the country. Name this artist who still teaches in Wilmington.
    a. Edward Loper
    b. Vincent Smith
    c. Edward Mitchell Bannister
    d. Joshua Johnson

26. This black educator was a Howard High School librarian and president of the Delaware NAACP. She also wrote a highly regarded chapter on local black history for H. C. Reed's *History of the First State* (1947) entitled "The Negro in Delaware: Past and Present." Who was she?
    a. Pauline A. Young
    b. Ida B. Wells
    c. Toni Morrison
    d. Rosa Parks

27. Name the Delaware historian who is noted for having edited *Delaware: A Guide to the First State* (1938)--a history written by Works Progress Administration writers.
    a. Jeannette Eckman
    b. Gertrude Crownfield
    c. Anne Parrish
    d. Anna T. Lincoln

28. This du Pont achieved a national reputation for her interest in horticulture. Who is she?
    a. Pamela du Pont Copeland
    b. Bessie Gardner du Pont
    c. Jessie Ball du Pont
    d. Helena Allaire Crozer du Pont

29. Although he is known primarily as an illustrator, Howard Pyle was also a successful writer. Name the title of the book he published in 1883 about Nottingham's famous fictional outlaw.
    a. *Jesse James*
    b. *Robin Hood*
    c. *Billy the Kid*
    d. *Al Capone*

30. Wilmington native John P. Marquand received a Pulitzer Prize for what novel in 1938?
    a. *The Late George Apley*
    b. *The Yearling*
    c. *The Grapes of Wrath*
    d. *Tales of the South Pacific*

31. During his tenure as the director of the Delaware Symphony, the symphony has achieved its greatest success. Name the conductor who is often invited to conduct other internationally known symphonies?
    a. Leopold Stokowski
    b. Steven Gunzenhauser
    c. Charles Munch
    d. Otto Klemperer

32. He made a living as a DuPont scientist, but entertained thousands as the Delaware Symphony Orchestra's principal violinist. Name the highly respected musician.
    a. Samuel Barber   c. Charles E. Ives
    b. Leo Ahramjian   d. Walter Piston

192

33. Wilmington's Diane Fratantoni is a Broadway success story. One of her roles included starring as Grizabella in the Broadway production of what musical?
    a. *Cats*
    b. *Damn Yankees*
    c. *Guys and Dolls*
    d. *Treemonisha*

34. Two sisters from Wilmington, Katherine and Kathleen have achieved international recognition as operatic singers. What is their last name?
    a. Heyde
    b. Ceisinski
    c. Jamison
    d. McDaniel

35. The Three Little Bakers Dinner Theatre was started by three brothers who achieved national show business success for which of the following?
    a. Broadway
    b. stand-up comedy
    c. acrobatics and tumbling
    d. singing

36. Theater lovers credit the artistic director and head of the Delaware Theater Company for bringing new life to theater in the state. Who is he?
    a. Cleveland Morris
    b. Patrick Mason
    c. Harold Prince
    d. David O. Selznick

37. Delaware dance legend James Jamieson brought out the best in his student dancers at Wilmington's Academy of the Dance. Jamieson himself received international acclaim for his role in a musical comedy which featured Scottish Highland dancing. What is the name of this musical?
    a. *Show Boat*
    b. *Cabaret*
    c. *Paint Your Wagon*
    d. *Brigadoon*

38. A poet who now teaches at the University of Delaware won a Pulitzer Prize in 1960 for his book of poems entitled *Heart's Needle*. Who is he?
    a. Gary Snyder
    b. W. D. Snodgrass
    c. Robert Lowell
    d. Richard Wilbur

39. Dr. Harry Shipman, a physics and astronomy professor at the University of Delaware, has an international reputation for his study of stars that are so condensed their gravitational field stops light from being emitted. What are these stars called?
    a. super novas
    b. black holes
    c. nebulas
    d. dwarfs

40. Name the Delaware historian and University of Delaware professor who wrote the 1977 publication *Delaware: A Bicentennial History*.
    a. Elizabeth Montgomery
    b. Anna T. Lincoln
    c. Carol E. Hoffecker
    d. Jeannette Eckman

41. This Wilmington City Council President paid tribute to black musicians in the 1989 publication, *The Genuine American Music*. Who wrote it?
    a. Leonard Feather
    b. Nat Hentoff
    c. James Baker
    d. August Wilson

42. This Widener College professor researched and wrote extensively about the Delaware Native Americans. Who was he?
    a. C. A. Weslager
    b. Henry C. Conrad
    c. Henry Seidel Canby
    d. Christopher L. Ward

43. This former Delaware Coast Press writer turned her interest in Sussex people and lore into a book, *Seagulls Hate Parsnips* (first edition published 1978). Who is she?
    a. Elaine Townsend Dickerson
    b. Nancy Steffens Seaman
    c. Virginia M. Tanzer
    d. Robin Brown

44. This historian's book, *History of Delaware*, was published in 1888 and is now considered a valuable collector's item. Who wrote this book?
    a. Amandus Johnson
    b. J. Thomas Scharf
    c. Benjamin Ferns
    d. George B. Rodney

45. A number of photographers, including Michael Biggs, Jake Riis, and Pat Crowe, have published books of Delaware photographs. Another photographer whose publications include the 1992 publication *Delaware Discovered* has worked for *National Geographic* and is a graduate of Smyrna High School. Name the photographer who now lives in Annapolis.
    a. Cathy Gruver
    b. Mary Erica Loewenstein
    c. Kevin Fleming
    d. Susan L. Gregg

46. Lewes artist Howard Schroeder received long overdue national recognition when he was featured on this television jounalist's Sunday morning program.
    a. Walter Cronkite
    b. Charles Kuralt
    c. Dan Rather
    d. Ted Koppel

The Creative Answers

1. c. Clifford Brown

2. b. Robert Lowery

3. d. Newport

4. d. Ernie Watts

5. a. The Destroyers

6. b. Verlaine

7. b. Allman Brothers

8. c. Bob Marley

9. b. Pepsi

10. c. F. Scott Fitzgerald

11. d. J. Saunders Redding

12. a. Bill Frank

13. b. Ralph Moyed

14. c. Jim Miller

15. c. Mary Ann Shadd Carey

16. b. Betty Burroughs

17. d. George Alfred Townsend

18. b. Valerie Bertinelli

19.   b.   Nancy Karibjanian

20.   c.   Jill Chernekoff

21.   d.   Ken Burns

22.   a.   Joe Pyne

23.   b.   Laura Branigan

24.   c.   Charles Parks

25.   a.   Edward Loper

26.   a.   Pauline A. Young

27.   a.   Jeannette Eckman

28.   a.   Pamela du Pont Copeland

29.   b.   _Robin Hood_

30.   a.   _The Late George Apley_

31.   b.   Steven Gunzenhauser

32.   b.   Leo Ahramjian

33.   a.   _Cats_

34.   b.   Ceisinski

35.   c.   acrobatics and tumbling

36.   a.   Cleveland Morris

37.   d.   _Brigadoon_

38. b. W. D. Snodgrass

39. b. black holes

40. c. Carol E. Hoffecker

41. c. James Baker

42. a. C. A. Weslager

43. c. Virginia M. Tanzer

44. b. J. Thomas Scharf

45. c. Kevin Fleming

46. b. Charles Kuralt

Sports Stars

1. Let's start with some Delawareans who have featured prominently as Phillies' stars. Who pitched for the Phillies and eventually managed the team to a 1980 World Series Championship?
   a. Dallas Green
   b. Jim Bunning
   c. Ryne Duren
   d. Gene Mauch

2. What Milford-born Phillies' pitcher won twenty games for them in 1966?
   a. Steve Carlton
   b. John Boozer
   c. Chris Short
   d. Dennis Bennett

3. This National Baseball Hall of Fame ballplayer played third base, had a .344 lifetime batting average in the Negro Leagues, and eventually served as a scout for the Phillies. Who was this Wilmington-born ballplayer?
   a. Jackie Robinson
   b. William "Judy" Johnson
   c. George Stovey
   d. Satchel Paige

4. "Harry the Horse" had his best major league year with the Phillies in 1958 when he hit .301. What is Harry's last name?
   a. Gonzalez
   b. Covington
   c. Averill
   d. Anderson

5. What Dickinson High graduate played ten years with the Detroit Tigers before ending his major league career with the Phillies?
   a. John Wockenfuss
   b. Johnny Callison
   c. Bobby Wine
   d. Bobby Shantz

6. Name the Delaware family that owned the Phillies when they won the 1980 World Series.
   a. du Pont
   b. Carpenter
   c. Bancroft
   d. Chipman

7. Delawarean Paul Richardson has been with the Phillies for many years, although he's never "taken the field." What does he do for the Phillies?
   a. official organist
   b. general manager
   c. Veterans Stadium manager
   d. ticket sales manager

8. Name the Delawarean who created the Phillie Phanatic and played the role for many years.
   a. Doug Henning
   b. Jim Henson
   c. Harry Blackstone, Jr.
   d. Dave Raymond

9. This second baseman, who began his professional career with the Montreal Expos, is now showing the country what he showed Seaford High School in the 1980s. Who is he?
   a. Mookie Wilson
   b. Delino Deshields
   c. Milt Thompson
   d. Roberto Alomar

10. Derrick May was a first round draft pick for the Chicago Cubs in 1986. Where did he go to high school?
    a. Brandywine
    b. Smyrna
    c. Seaford
    d. Newark

11. Middletown High graduate Dwayne Henry played for a number of major league teams in what position?
    a. first base
    b. center field
    c. catcher
    d. pitcher

12. Name the figure skating pair who trained in Newark and who competed in the 1994 Winter Olympics.
    a. Courtland and Reynolds
    b. Gordeeva and Grinkow
    c. Torvill and Dean
    c. Valova and Vassiliev

13. Concord High School and University of Delaware graduate Audie Kujala Showalter was inducted into the Delaware Sports Hall of Fame in 1992 because of her athletic prowess in field hockey and another sport that she played professionally in Connecticut. What is this sport?
    a. tennis   c. volleyball
    b. softball   d. basketball

14. In 1993, Delaware Sports Hall of Fame inductee Milt Roberts was recognized for starting the first public school lacrosse program in Delaware (started in 1979). At what Sussex County school did Roberts begin the program?
    a. Sussex Central Senior High
    b. Seaford High
    c. Indian River High
    d. Cape Henlopen High

15. Local engineer Frank Masley competed in the Olympics three times. In what sport did he compete?
    a. speed skating
    b. luge
    c. figure skating
    d. bobsled

16. The resurgence of the Wilmington Blue Rocks in 1993, Delaware's minor league baseball team, caused a great deal of excitement. Delaware also has a professional soccer team that debuted in 1993. What is its name?
    a. Blue Bombers
    b. Blue Hens
    c. Wizards
    d. Freedom

17. The Blue Rocks are a minor league team for what organization?
    a. Mets
    b. Phillies
    c. Royals
    d. Dodgers

18. In the 1980s, three University of Delaware quarterbacks played in the NFL--all of whom are listed below. Which one of the following did not play at the University of Delaware?
    a. Rudy Bukich
    b. Scott Bruner
    c. Jeff Komo
    d. Rich Gannon

19. What Delawarean had a remarkable career as a defensive lineman for the Dallas Cowboys?
    a. Randy White
    b. Herschel Walker
    c. Tony Dorsett
    d. Jethro Pugh

20. Brothers Conway and Gary, Newark High athletes, had successful careers as professional football players and were both inducted into the Delaware Sports Hall of Fame. What is their last name?
    a. Carpenter
    b. Wills
    c. Hayman
    d. Swann

21. Thousands turned out in 1967 to see Newark High School beat an "unbeatable" team coached by the legendary Bill Billings who took his team to a 53-game winning streak his first five seasons. Name the school Billings coached for.
    a. Laurel High
    b. Dover High
    c. Smyrna High
    d. Middletown High

22. Ursuline basketball star Val Whiting went on to achieve national recognition for her skills at Stanford University. In recognition of her success the Basketball Hall of Fame displays her jersey. Where is the Hall of Fame located?
    a. Springfield, Massachusetts
    b. Detroit, Michigan
    c. Atlanta, Georgia
    d. Canton, Ohio

23. St. Mark's graduate Steve Watson played ten years in the NFL and considers it one of the highlights of his career to have played against the Giants in the 1987 Superbowl. Who did Watson play for?
    a. Dallas Cowboys
    b. Philadelphia Eagles
    c. Miami Dolphins
    d. Denver Broncos

24. Dave Tiberi's biography provides more convincing evidence that he was "robbed" of the title in 1992. At what weight class did Tiberi fight?
    a. heavyweight
    b. light-heavyweight
    c. supermiddle weight
    d. welterweight

25. Delaware fighter, Henry Milligan, won the 1983 National Amateur Heavyweight Championship. Milligan lost a 1984 Olympic trials bout when he faced a future professional heavyweight champion. Whom did Milligan face?
    a. Mike Tyson
    b. Joe Frazier
    c. Ken Norton
    d. George Foreman

26. Name the fighter (now a Greenville resident) who defeated Larry Holmes in 1985 for the IBF world heavyweight title.
    a. James "Buster" Douglas
    b. Thomas Hearns
    c. Ken Norton
    d. Michael Spinks

27. Light heavyweight Art Redden was a Howard High graduate who posted an impressive 65-6 career record after taking up boxing as a Marine. Redden fought on the 1968 American Olympic team which included which well-known heavyweight?
    a. Muhammad Ali   c. Leon Spinks
    b. Rocky Marciano   d. George Foreman

28. One of the best runners to come from Delaware, she finished 6th in the 1988 Olympics in the 3,000 meters. Who is she?
    a. Rita Justice
    b. Jackie Pitts
    c. Gretchen Spruance
    d. Vicki Huber

29. Tubby Raymond perfected the Winged-T offense, but credit should be given to Raymond's mentor who developed the football offense for the University of Delaware. Name the former coach and athletic director.
   a. Paul Bryant
   b. Dave Nelson
   c. Glenn Warner
   d. Eddie Robinson

30. After a spectacular season in 1991-92, the University of Delaware basketball team earned its first appearance in the NCAA. Name the coach who guided the team to success.
   a. John Wooden
   b. Steve Steinwedel
   c. Adolph Rupp
   d. Rollie Massimino

31. From 1986 to 1992, the girls basketball team of this private school ruled the hoops by winning six of seven state championships. Name the school.
   a. Archmere
   b. St. Mark's
   c. Padua
   d. Ursuline

32. Under the guidance of Bill Collick, the Delaware State Hornets have achieved football success by winning or sharing the Mid-Eastern Athletic Conference title a number of times. What is the name of the stadium where the Hornets play football?
   a. Alumni
   b. Redding
   c. Brown
   d. Jason

33. Since 1986, it has proven hard to beat this private school soccer powerhouse who, under the direction of Coach Tom DeMatteis, has won the state championship many times. Name the school.
    a. St. Mark's
    b. Salesianum
    c. Tower Hill
    d. Sanford

34. Bob Tattersall has coached high school football longer than any other coach in Delaware. Where does Coach Tattersall coach?
    a. Wilmington High
    b. Tower Hill
    c. Wilmington Friends
    d. Milford

35. Name the Howard Career Center graduate and 1986 Delaware Player of the Year who played guard for the Washington Bullets.
    a. George Mikan
    b. Oscar Robinson
    c. Bill Bradley
    d. A. J. English

36. Bill Passmore rode 3,533 winners in his career. In what sport did Passmore compete?
    a. harness racing
    b. thoroughbred racing

37. Unfortunately many Delaware women athletes and coaches don't get the recognition they deserve because their sports don't get as much media attention and fan participation as men's sports. A prime example, Nancy Churchman Sawin-- coach, educator, and artist--deserves a great deal of credit for her devotion to what girls' sport?
    a. basketball
    b. tennis
    c. field hockey
    d. gymnastics

38. Izzy Katzman, Al Cartwright, and John Brady were inducted into the Delaware Sports Hall of Fame even though none of them is noted for coaching or playing a sport. Why were they inducted?
     a.   for their sports writing and editing
     b.   because they were team owners
     c.   because of their sponsorship of sports
     d.   for their sports announcing

Sports Stars Answers

1.   a.   Dallas Green

2.   c.   Chris Short

3.   b.   William "Judy" Johnson

4.   d.   Anderson

5.   a.   John Wockenfuss

6.   b.   Carpenter

7.   a.   official organist

8.   d.   Dave Raymond

9.   b.   Delino Deshields

10.   d.   Newark

11.   d.   pitcher

12.   a.   Courtland and Reynolds

13.   b.   softball

14.   d.   Cape Henlopen High

15.   b.   luge

16.   c.   Wizards

17.   c.   Royals

18.   a.   Rudy Bukich

19.   a.   Randy White

20.   c.   Hayman

21.   d.   Middletown High

22.   a.   Springfield, Massachusetts

23.   d.   Denver Broncos

24.   c.   supermiddle weight

25.   a.   Mike Tyson

26.   d.   Michael Spinks

27.   d.   George Foreman

28.   d.   Vicki Huber

29.   b.   Dave Nelson

30.   b.   Steve Steinwedel

31.   d.   Ursuline

32.   a.   Alumni

33.   a.   St. Mark's

34.   c.   Wilmington Friends

35.   d.   A. J. English

36.   b.   thoroughbred racing

37.   c.   field hockey

38.   a.   for their sports writing and editing

Sources

Biggs, Mike and Barbara Benson. *Wilmington: The City and Beyond.* 1991

Bryant, Tracey L. and Jonathan R. Pennock, eds. *The Delaware Estuary: Rediscovering a Forgotten Resource.* 1988

Delaware Heritage Commission. *A Legacy From Delaware Women.* 1987

Dolan, Paul and James R. Soles. *Government of Delaware.* 1976

Eberlein, Harold Donaldson and Cortlandt V. D. Hubbard. *Historic Houses and Buildings of Delaware.* 1962

Eckman, Jeannette, ed. *Delaware: A Guide to the First State.* 1955

Frank, Bill. *Delaware: Six Decades through the Eyes of a Working Newspaperman.* 1987

Hancock, Harold B. *A History of Kent County.* 1976

Hancock, Harold B. *A History of Sussex County.* 1976

Hancock, Harold B. *The Delaware State During the American Revolution.* 1976

Hoffecker, Carol E. *Delaware, the First State.* 1988

Hoffecker, Carol E. *Delaware: A Bicentennial History.* 1977

Macdonald, Betty Harrington. *Historic Landmarks of Delaware and the Eastern Shore.* 1963

Martin, Roger A. *A History of Delaware Through its Governors, 1776-1984.* 1984

Munroe, John A. *History of Delaware.* 1984

Reed, H. Clay, ed. *Delaware: A History of the First State.* 1947

Robinson, Robert H. *Visiting Sussex Even If You Live Here.* 1976

Ryan, Elizabeth H. ed. *Delaware Government: All You Ever Wanted to Know About Government and Didn't Know Where to Ask!* 1991

Scharf, J. Thomas. *A History of Delaware.* 1888

Sunday *News Journal* Editors. *A Delaware Almanac: Newcomers Guide.* 1988

Ward, Mary Sam, ed. *Delaware Women Remembered.* 1977

Williams, William Henry. *An Illustrated History of Delaware.* 1985

Papers and Magazines

Delaware Coastal Press

Delaware History

Delaware Lawyer

Delaware State News

Delaware Today

News Journal Papers

Outdoor Delaware

About the Author

Alexander "Sandy" Shalk is a graduate of Christiana High School and the University of Delaware--both in Newark, Delaware. He began his teaching career at Smyrna High School, in Smyrna, Delaware, where he taught English and social studies. At present, he is an assistant principal at Milford High School in Milford, Delaware, and resides in Lewes, Delaware, with his wife Christine and son Benjamin.

Del
917.51
SHA

Shalk, Alexander

Delaware, a trivia guide
to the First State

MAR 09 1998	**DATE DUE**		
APR 20 1998			
APR 20 1998			
DEC 05 2000			
MAY 24 2002			
SEP 29			
OCT 19			